Let There

CREATING A LIFE WORTH LIVING

By Dr. Demetrius S. Carolina, Sr.

A NON-FICTION IMPRINT FROM ADDUCENT
Adducent, Inc.
www.Adducent.Co

<u>Titles Distributed In</u>
North America
United Kingdom
Western Europe
South America
Australia

Let There Be Light

CREATING A LIFE WORTH LIVING

By Dr. Demetrius S. Carolina, Sr.

Let There Be Light

Creating A Life Worth Living

By Dr. Demetrius S. Carolina, Sr.

Hardback: ISBN 978-1-937592-19-6

Paperback: ISBN 978-1-937592-20-2

A Fortis book published by Adducent

Jacksonville, Florida

www.Adducent.Co

Published in the United States of America

Illustrations by (and courtesy of) Ian Coate, www.IanCoate.com.

Table of Contents

Dedication

One can accomplish little in this life that is worthwhile without the love and support of others. It is my joy to have a wonderful team of supporters that encourage, challenge and keep me in prayer.

I dedicate this book to my family:

Bernice, my wife and Dior, DeLisa and Demetrius II, my children; Tiffany, Cyani and Demetrius my God-children; to my FCBC church family; to Mrs. Dolores Carolina-McKinsey, my loving mother; to Mrs. Minnie North and Mother Lizzie Alexander my spiritual advisors and to the memory of Willie and Hazel Carolina, my grandparents and two of the wisest people I have known.

There are, of course, many people who have poured into my life and to you I am grateful as fruits of your efforts are still becoming evident.

To God goes the glory because the best is yet to come!

Acknowledgments

No one and no profession has been given the gift to affect positive change in the lives of other as much as educators. They have the power to teach you to invest in yourself.

I will ever be indebted to Mrs. Paul, my second grade reading teacher, who accepted nothing but my best and pulled excellence from me. She showed me what others failed to see in me; a leader, someone worth investing in and a man of substance and integrity. Thanks to you Mrs. Paul, reading specialist at Winslow 1 Elementary School, your ministry of education has reached the world.

Talent and skill is developed over time and must be nurtured by those who have an eye to see what others miss. Dennis M. Lowery is a gifted, insightful and talented artist, who is able to listen and can hear what is intended (a rare skill) and has the talent to create masterpieces out of fragmented ideas. Thanks, Dennis, for sharing your gifts with the world.

Lastly, the world is becoming smaller daily. With the advancement of various technologies the way in which we communicate has changed tremendously. We can reach out and witness the actions of others around the world in real time. While this is an exciting time in which to be alive it is also a challenging time. We are witnessing hyper-change within governments, cities and towns around the world. The way in which we communicate with others comes with greater results and consequences. It is my sincere hope that this book is a vehicle for effecting positive meaningful change in the lives of its readers from the inside out, whether through printed versions, e-book or audio versions. Technological advance has afforded me and others many means to share God's gift with the world.

At the Beginning

"Alice came to a fork in the road. 'Which road do I take?' she asked. 'Where do you want to go?' responded the Cheshire cat.

'I don't know,' Alice answered. 'Then,' said the cat, 'it doesn't matter.'"

-Lewis Carroll, Alice in Wonderland

Think about this.

Who, ultimately, is responsible for your life?

You—of course!

And "You" are the biggest commitment you'll ever make in life.

For the rest of your life to "work well"... and for you to be able to help others... you have to focus on yourself first.

But, in order to do that, we all need help and guidance along the way.

And that is the purpose of this book... to offer practical guidance on how to get from where you are to where you want to be in your spiritual life. And we all know that what is in our heads and hearts can be manifested in the real world.

What you will take away from this book is the importance of how the things you control are the key in creating a life worth living and having a relationship with yourself and others that is fulfilling and sustainable... one that can last... forever.

* * *

I have served others as a counselor, pastor, teacher, leader and friend for many years. In that time I have seen good people, who were well intentioned, go through life—just getting by—existing rather than truly living it to the fullest. There are many reasons for this situation; the most prominent being that human beings are creatures of habit. We are most comfortable with what we are most familiar.

Left on our own, it's often very hard to make changes to improve our lot in life. In fact, for many it's hard to even pinpoint what's really wrong without some sort of outside stimulus—some prod—that goads us to evaluate or assess ourselves. And while everybody is responsible for their own lives; it certainly helps to have something or someone that becomes a catalyst to break through your life routine and be the "kick in the pants" needed to take action.

Life is short and too often many have a voice inside that says, "I wish I had...," or "If I only...," or worse it's whispering to you, "You're just not good enough... not smart enough...." The voice in and of itself is not a terrible thing. I believe all humans have heard it inside their head at some point. The tragedy is when that voice becomes a constant—never ending—drumbeat in your head that becomes a question you can't answer or a statement that you can't refute. It becomes something you believe about yourself that is only true if you let it become true.

I just shared with you something that is worth an incalculable amount of money if you take it to heart. *Things, bad and good, become true only if you let, or make, them come true.*

In this book we'll talk about ways to stop that voice, to answer the nagging questions and refute mental statements that just aren't true.

The Three Fs that can empower you

Fear(s), Frustration(s), and Failing(s) can serve as stepping stones towards a better you. I know this from personal experience.

I was told as a young child that I would not excel academically. I had a disability that others thought meant I just wasn't capable. I just wasn't smart enough or good enough to do well in school. I had (have), at that time, a little known learning deficiency called Dyslexia.

It was my mother Dolores Carolina-McKinsey who insisted that I remain in mainstream classes and that additional support was provided to aid me in the learning process. But it was my special support teacher Ms. Paul who told me something I have held close all these years through high school graduation, undergraduate school and a doctoral degree program: Be proud of who you are and where you are! Use that to be more... to do more.

You are more capable than anyone thinks if you believe in yourself.

We all have the ability to become more but we have to make the connection between hope, belief and action. Hope by itself is simply a dream. There must be a level of belief attached to hopes and dreams to motivate action on the part of the believer.

Hope is an attitude, a desire that rests solely in our head or perhaps our heart. But it does no good if that's where it remains. If one truly believes in something, believes in a goal or destination; he or she will do what is necessary to work towards it. And as you work to make it a reality you build anticipation for it and envision reaching or accomplishing it in time. It is not easy to explain but when we believe in something we often act in illogical ways to others but very logical to ourselves. Having the inspiration and audacity to act on a belief is what allowed the pilgrims to press forward to come to a new land. Acting upon what was felt to be right is what empowered the Civil Rights Movement, the Protestant Reformation and the Tiananmen Square resistance. Acting on and believing in what was right brought down the Berlin Wall and many more obstacles to freedom and liberty. There is an indelible link between hope, belief and action.

* * *

Working as a college administrator and educator in what was at the time the fifth poorest city in the nation, I experienced the transformation manifested through self-empowerment. It can take a person from a system of repression and a mindset of dependency and set them free.

One of the things I loved about my job was not apparent to me at first, but I realized and came to appreciate (and cherish) it over time. I had the opportunity to see students come in one way; young, perhaps naïve and uncertain but leave matured and better equipped to face the greater challenges life will present them. I was in a position to see many people come through the door carrying not just their books or possessions but most important their dreams, hopes and the potential that all humans have inside. All of whom simply needed the appropriate support and direction to transform into the person, leader, and perhaps one day even the mentor they desired to become. Of course everyone did not succeed. Just showing up does not mean you win or get a prize in life. However, everyone did receive the opportunity to succeed and that is what we should expect from life—the chance to take full measure and become all that we wish to be. It's within the power of all of us to make happen.

One of life's affirming truths are we will always have opportunities to give and to receive. It is the wisest people who can distinguish the time when it is necessary to do one or the other and to seize opportunities as they are presented. There are also times when we have the great gift of making opportunities available to others. Those times are rare and must be treasured.

* * *

I was brought up in rural community where everyone knew each other and where I had many mothers and extended family. In a way I became accountable to many people. Since that is something you are always aware of in such an environment it creates an almost continual subconscious appraisal of your behavior and actions. As I grew older that turned into moments of reflection and introspection. And as life can be so very busy, those moments are the most valuable to me and I hope that as you read this book you will develop that habit for yourself.

It is important to pause, to take a moment and reflect from time to time just to gain a clearer perspective on where you are in life. Reflection allows you to evaluate your successes and failures but you don't want to dwell on one to the exclusion of the other as both are helpful for holistic growth. We learn from the good and the bad in our life. If one of your dreams or desires is to have a better life you must look at what actions (or inactions) led you to where you are and adjust your thinking and belief system to empower you to get to where you want to go.

Reflection and thought ensures you don't remain in a holding pattern. It's when we fail to think, to look deeply at things... that we end up in limbo. Our life going nowhere and getting there too fast.

Too often we spin our wheels on people, places and things that have little positive impact upon our lives and fail to redirect our energies towards more fruitful endeavors. We become burned out and miss meaningful opportunities for growth and change.

We all have only one life and each day in it has 24 hours (the same amount for the rich, the poor, the happy, the sad and everyone on this earth in between). It's what you do with your time that counts.

But your life is not set to a pre-determined unalterable course. You can change it based on the decisions you make as your journey continues. Taking time to reflect can give you (or define for you) choices and alter outcomes. Just think how different one's life can become and how that one life can impact the world around it when you begin living life instead of letting life live you.

* * *

The advances of technology has made the world smaller and what was once so far away is now closer... and I believe people are more aware of each other. What occurs on one side of the earth can be viewed and often reacted to in real time by others around the world. This has helped us all to discover daily, as human beings, what makes us human, what we have in common and to think about the intrinsic values of our life regardless of who we are and where we live. And it makes more visible the shared stories of those who have less than we do but were able to do more (it's more of a qualitative comparison than quantity). Seeing what other's do or have done despite challenges, despite heartache and frustration is inspirational and gives all of us hope that we can do more with what we have. Or to find what we need to do what we must do for ourselves, our families and our communities and that is an important part of letting light come into our lives.

Chapter 1

What Are You Seeking
(and what should you seek)?

"And now here is my secret, a very simple
secret; it is only with the heart that one can
see rightly, what is essential is invisible to the
eye."

-The Little Prince (by Antoine de Saint-Exupéry)

Every day most of us think about what we're going to feed
our body.

We think about the food and drink that we like... we have preferences and choices and often (especially with spouses and family) there is discussion or contemplation, "What are we (am I) having for dinner?" or "What do (I) you want for dinner?" There's even a little bit of entertainment value to planning for the meal. It's part of daily life.

But what are we (you) feeding our (your) mind?

Isn't your mental diet just as important as the physical one that fuels your body?

Isn't what goes through your mind and what it leaves behind just as important as the calories you consume that your body keeps a bit of before burning?

The answer to the above two questions is: YES

But many people, so caught up or busy with life, don't— and I mean this literally—give it a second thought. We truly don't think about "thinking"... about giving our mind the right fuel to burn that will get us to the place we want to be in life.

Think for yourself and shake the dust off the real dreams and aspirations you have and give active thought to how to move towards achieving them even if it means only small steps a day at a time.

We are all looking for something... but vague dreams and notions won't help you. You must clearly identify what important goals you have for your life. And then—and this is very important—sit down and define what you are doing to reach them. What is your life plan? Write out your vision. Write out positive affirmations on your calendar. Start to develop a daily diet of thought to strengthen how you feel about yourself in your own mind. Work on the things where you know you are weak and do what you need to do to eliminate that weakness. Surround yourself with purpose and definition of what you want to do and how you are going to do it.

Life is aimless (and often fruitless) without goals to strive for or a star to steer by. Equally important or perhaps even more so is your identity and mission. And those are found solely inside your own thoughts.

A section of the Bible that is particularly apt is worth discussing here:

WHAT BREAD ARE YOU SEEKING, JOHN 6:25-40

> When they found him on the other side of the lake, they asked, "Rabbi, when did you get here?"
>
> Jesus answered, "I tell you the truth, and you are looking for me, not because you saw miraculous signs but because you ate the loaves and had your fill. Do not work for food that spoils, but for food that endures to eternal life, which the Son of Man will give you. On him God the Father has placed his seal of approval."
>
> Then they asked him, "What must we do to do the works God requires?"
>
> Jesus answered, "The work of God is this: to believe in the one he has sent."

So they asked him, "What miraculous sign then will you give that we may see it and believe you? What will you do? Our forefathers ate the manna in the desert; as it is written: 'He gave them bread from heaven to eat.'"

Jesus said to them, "I tell you the truth, it is not Moses who has given you the bread from heaven, but it is my Father who gives you the true bread from heaven. For the bread of God is he who comes down from heaven and gives life to the world."

"Sir," they said, "from now on give us this bread."

Then Jesus declared, "I am the bread of life. He who comes to me will never go hungry, and he who believes in me will never be thirsty. But as I told you, you have seen me and still you do not believe. All that the Father gives me will come to me, and whoever comes to me I will never drive away. For I have come down from heaven not to do my will but to do the will of him who sent me. And this is the will of him who sent me that I shall lose none of all that he has given me, but raise them up at the last day. For my Father's will is that everyone who looks to the Son and

believes in him shall have eternal life, and I will
raise him up at the last day."

The Capernaum discourse (6:22–59) is an open and candid discussion by Jesus concerning His identity and mission. In the text we find the crowd questioning Jesus as to how He is going to prove Himself to them yet again (after feeding 5000 people with a few loaves and fish). Isn't it amazing how we look for miracles while we often miss the fact that everyday all around us they constantly occur.

You see, the crowd needed food and Jesus saw and met the need.

They'd followed Jesus all the way around the lake. They were highly motivated to have a PERCEIVED need met, but did not recognize that they were being offered the solution to the REAL need in their lives.

Jesus reminded them of the importance of what He was offering them and then attempts to teach them what their REAL NEED was rather than meeting their perceived need for food. He was speaking of their eternal need and they only were concerned with earthly provision and prosperity. It shows how shortsighted people can be.

In order to speak to the need of a person you have to know the circumstances of the person.

[Jesus is in the synagogue (6:59), and its Passover. The Jewish community has been studying the Scriptures that pertain to the departure from Egypt (through the sea) and the flight into the desert. Jesus uses the images of Passover that they understood well. First He taught that He is the Bread of Life out of heaven.] You do know in the wilderness God rained down bread from Heaven for the Israelites. The first type of Bread we see Him to be is sustaining bread.

And not aware that Jesus had walked across the lake they ask in verse 25; when they found Him on the other side of the sea, "Rabbi, when did You get here?"

The initial question is about how Jesus arrived since He had not gotten in His disciples' boat. Jesus takes the crowd's question as having two-levels, one material (He came by boat) and another spiritual (He came from heaven) 6:33; 7:28.

Jesus turns the discussion of His feeding miracle to that of a much higher concern. In verse 26 He helps them understand the deeper meaning of feed a person for a day versus providing them with blessed assurance for this life and the life yet to come!

He says "Truly, truly, I say to you, you seek Me, not because you saw signs, but because you ate of the loaves and were filled. So Jesus criticized the people who followed Him only for the physical and temporal benefits and not for the satisfying of their spiritual hunger.

Many people use religion to gain prestige, comfort, acceptance or even political votes. But those are self-centered motives. Verse 27 is Jesus' reply to the materialism of mankind. "Do not work for the food which perishes, but for the food which endures to eternal life, which the Son of Man will give to you, for on Him the Father, God, has set His seal." Isn't it good to know that Spiritual assurance covers what earthly insurance leaves out?!

As Jesus teaches in the synagogue, He desires to lift His hearers above a humanistic understanding of His miracle. He argues that their efforts should be focused not on the loaves and fish, but on the higher substance that lasts forever. "Man does not live on bread alone, but on every word that comes from the mouth of God" (Mt. 4:4). Physical food is short-lived but spiritual food leads to eternal life. The Son of Man will give people this spiritual food, which is ultimately Christ Himself (6:53). It was not the gift that is important, but the Giver (Jesus, the Son of Man), on whom God has set His seal.

Have you been putting all of your energies into getting ahead in this world while neglecting what is the most important thing?

Have you been seeking the wrong bread?

Jesus said, "Do not labor for the food which perishes, but for the food which endures to everlasting life" (Jn. 6:27).

The people were looking for Jesus, but they were not looking for the right reason. They did not know what they really needed yet because they could not lift their minds above the physical needs of life.

I know we all need food, clothing and shelter. I also know we all desire to live a comfortable existence and some of us have many things that we believe are what we need. We think that they are indeed the "food", the "bread" of life.

But who needs a big house without love in it?

What does it mean to have a lot of money and still feel there is a void in your life?

I know that there are even worse situations that people may find themselves in:

Not enough money to pay the bills.

Not enough food to feed their family.

Not enough time, too busy working to spend needed time with their spouse, family and friends.

Just not enough...

So we seek answers. We seek out who can show us the way. And I'm telling you that the best person to lead you is yourself. You just need to focus on the right things. On finding the right "bread" for your mind, heart and soul.

THE TRUE BREAD OF HEAVEN 30-32

Verse 30 reveals that they finally understood Jesus was asking them to believe in Him. So they said to Him, "What then do You do for a sign, so that we may see, and believe You? What work do You perform?

They thought God's order was to see and believe.

But the divine order, what comes first, is to believe and then you will see (John 11:40).

This is true in the real as well as spiritual world. It is what we believe inside that ultimately leads to (or manifests) what we see with our eyes and can feel with our hands.

THE BREAD OF LIFE 33-35

The bread God supplies gives life. "For the bread of God is the One who comes down out of heaven, and gives life to the world."

The "bread" I feel that is most important to us as human being is... **"Belief"**

More on that shortly but first most of us realize that certain types of creation require heat, friction and upheaval.

Bread dough rises when heat is put to it. Fire starts through the striking of two materials to create a spark that ignites. Mountains are created from the upheaval of the very ground beneath us.

You might ask, "What does that have to do with me. How is it relevant to belief?"

Because to fill the absence of belief often takes one of those catalysts (and there are others, too) to bring about change. The heat and pressure of life... the creative spark we must strike when we cry out for help... should goad us to make changes in our life. And change can create something within that becomes:

- your light in the darkness;
- your security in times of uncertainty;
- your companion in loneliness;
- your guide when you are lost;
- your protector in battle;
- your hope in life;
- your certainty when you become confused, and
- your source of vitality for productiveness.

He desires that we should receive Him not only for what He might give us, but for what He might be to us and in us. So the "bread" that you seek; the very thing that bonds your mind, heart and soul together to work for your benefit; the very thing that you need most in life; is: **Belief**

In yourself; in creating a better life and in finding the things that truly make you happy. When you believe you can... you will see how.

Chapter 2

We Are Not Alone

"What is the appropriate behavior for a man
or a woman in the midst of this world, where
each person is clinging to his piece of debris?
What's the proper salutation between people
as they pass each other in this flood? "

-Buddha

Part of establishing a strong core of personal belief is
realizing that even when you feel lonely and disconnected;
when you face difficult times and it seems no one is on
your side; you are not alone.

All of us have our troubles to bear and challenges to face. The nature of being human is to experience the joys of success, happiness and love but also know, and deal with, disappointment, despair and loneliness. What you feel is what others feel or have felt relevant to their own experience.

It has often been said that the true test of a person's character and strength is demonstrated in the worst of times. If you really want to know what a person is made of walk with them through hardship and crisis.

I know this to be true and believe we grow the most in times of adversity and struggle. While no one wants to go through hard times and difficult circumstances, we often come through them as a better person and certainly stronger. We tend to be more understanding of others, more patient and tolerant and better equipped for leadership and relationships. We mature as we persevere to make it through the storms that occur in every person's life.

It is during those times that we most often feel alone. Tunnel-vision sets in and all we can see is the black walls of what is going on in or with our life. It's hard to believe a light will ever shine on us again when you are deep in the pit. Everyone feels that way at different points during critical times. The important thing is to not fixate on that and to believe that things can and will change (back to the importance of belief, again).

But everyone experiences failure. It's how we deal with it that determines our future and we all must realize that it is in times of doubt, pressure and stress we grow the most.

The Bible speaks of us (Man) being like gold. In its purest state it is unpolished and almost unrecognizable (to those who don't know what to look for). But when it is mined from the ground and then processed and refined it becomes a most valuable commodity. To use another example: diamonds are created by heat and pressure and the end result is something that still does not look like much until it is cut and polished. So these things that are often buried and unrecognizable left alone have little value. It's only when someone finds and works with them that they become the type of treasure that many seek. Our souls are like that too.

Life teaches us that the art of refinement, for minerals and Man, is not an act of individuality. We grow and are made better through our interactions. Times in which the reality of our interconnectedness is made more evident and our vulnerabilities are revealed can be the most important times in our life. But we have to choose to let the loneliness go and open our eyes to our world and the people around us that can not only bring out and refine the value and worthiness of our lives... but can also help heal a wounded soul. We are alone only if we choose to be.

And though we are not alone... that doesn't mean using others as a scapegoat for our troubles and problems. Personal growth and development can and often does vary from person to person. But I'm sure we can all agree that growth refers to one's ability to do better, want something different, and operate from a more informed perspective and an important part of that is the ability to take responsibility for yourself. Owning your life and cleaning up behind yourself. Acknowledging and asking for forgiveness for the wrongs you have done. These are part of opening the door to the world, to let a life come in, which will remove the loneliness.

It is important to have a discussion with yourself regarding the need to assume responsibility for your life. The reality of your world centers within you. You have to understand and acknowledge that each individual life matters. Your life matters.

The way we live each day, good or bad, right, wrong or indifferently... matters.

How we make choices and their quality, matters.

These are the cornerstones of our existence and make up the sum and substance of our life. They must be treated with that level and degree of importance. When we respect things (or people) we tend to pay attention to them—they're important or in some way valuable to us. Our time and the way we make decisions are things we must have the highest respect for.

What we build for ourselves and our loved ones are all manifestations of our own internal reality and that reality must include venerating the very things that can help us.

But we can't fault others for the decisions we make. Everyone has had difficult times and experiences in life, some of which we bring on ourselves. It happens. No one is perfect and no one is exempt from trouble, problems or pain whether they are self-inflicted, unintentional or beyond our control. Accept responsibility for yourself and move on to make things better.

What you do with every day of your life, the way in which you use your past to handle the present, and how you treat others around you speaks to your character. No excuse can be made for one's character. It is who you are. But if who you are is not who you want to be—if what your life is, is not what you want—then you can change yourself and your life. But you need help to do that. You cannot do it solely.

The wonderful human experience afforded to all of us includes forgiveness, caring and self-sacrifice. These are actions that go beyond self-interest. These are actions that we bestow on others because they matter. These are actions that are the epitome of a belief that, "We truly are not alone."

In order to love we must consciously be part of the interconnected links in an unending chain of meaningful interactions. These interactions are important whether we realize it or not. It is an unchangeable fact we need each other. No one can live independent of others no matter the amount of self-reliance, intestinal fortitude or resources one may have.

Relationships

1 John 4:8 and 16 tells us, "God is love." Therefore, from eternity past and into eternity future God has always existed in an intimate loving relationship because love is the very nature of God. Before there was time the Father has always loved the Son and the Spirit; the Son has loved the Father and Spirit; the Spirit has loved the Father and the Son. And when time is no more each will continue to share an eternal love relationship with each other.

Have you ever wondered why God created the universe? Why did God make the earth the way it is; why did He create man? I don't pretend to know all the reasons, but I believe that creation is an expression of God's love. Love cannot be kept to oneself; real love must find expression. We can enjoy the wonders of God's creation because He loves us, but I think it goes even deeper than God's love for us.

And I think that love, in part, comes from a sense of togetherness and willingness to live your life in the open with an understanding that we don't make this journey of life alone (whether physically or spiritually).

Now again, I don't pretend to have it all figured out, but I believe that creation (and God's plan of salvation) is an expression of love both GOD to GOD and GOD to MAN. God is love and He has expressed His love in so many wonderful ways through creation and His plan of salvation.

Now think about this: God has made man; both male and female, in His image. Each of us has been made LIKE GOD. Therefore, one of the ways we have been made like God is that we too can share in loving relationships; like God we can give and receive love. When you experience God's love for you, when the love for your spouse is expressed, when you know the joy of your child or grandchild's love for you, when a friend shows you compassion—in these and countless other ways in which you can give and receive love—it is all because God made you to be like Him.

WE ARE MOST LIKE GOD WHEN WE GIVE LOVE TO OTHERS.

Love is selflessness; thinking not about yourself, but thinking first of those you love.

Genesis 2:18, 20-22

The Lord God said, "It is not good for the man to be alone. I will make a helper suitable for him." But for Adam no suitable helper was found. [this was NOT GOOD.] So the Lord God caused the man to fall into a deep sleep; and while he was sleeping, he took one of the man's ribs and closed up the place with flesh. Then the Lord God made a woman from the rib he had taken from the man, and He brought her to the man.

God said this was not good for man to be alone. God fashioned the woman from man; she is flesh of his flesh and bone of his bone. Eve was Adam's suitable helper; a counterpart of himself, one formed from his person, bearing his resemblance. Man and woman are made for each other. God does not intend for man to be alone; we are made to be in relationship with one another—and to relate (connect) to one another.

Ecclesiastes 4:9-10

Two are better than one, because they have a good return for their work: If one falls down, his friend can help him up. Pity the man who falls and has no one to help him!

American culture increasingly tries to isolate individuals from one another. We have pseudo relationships with characters on TV and in the movies; we watch them interact, while we are alone. We may chat on our computers, using a screen name or avatar, with someone far away, but we won't go next door to talk to our neighbors.

God would say that all of this is not good and frankly we as human beings would also say that, done to an extreme, living in a world without connecting at a personal and direct level, is not good for us. We are made to be in relationship with one another and to physically meet and interact with others. It's where our humanity comes from. How then has God designed human relationships? How should we relate to each other?

REMEMBER: WE ARE MOST LIKE GOD WHEN WE GIVE LOVE TO OTHERS.

If we are going to relate to each other as God intended, then our relationships must be built upon the foundation of love.

In Matthew 22:37-40 Jesus said that the greatest commandment was that we should love the Lord our God with all our heart, soul and mind. The second greatest is love your neighbors as yourself. Therefore, God's expectation—and His design—is that we relate to one another (and God) with love.

John 13:15 I have set you an example that you should do as I have done for you.

Jesus is our example of the perfect F.R.I.E.N.D. This is by no means an exhaustive list of relational skills, but all our relationships will benefit if we can begin to master these six things which Jesus modeled for us.

[F] A friend is **Forgiving**:

Jesus came to restore broken relationships; we too should forgive one another. Perhaps one of the best examples of how Jesus showed us how to forgive, restoring broken relationships, was with one of His very closest friends Peter in & John 21:15-17. To err is human; to forgive is divine. As God restores His image within us, He will enable us to forgive. All of us have experienced the pain of broken relationships; forgiveness sets us free to receive God's healing. "Love keeps no record of wrongs."

[R] A friend is **Real**:

Jesus did not compromise who he was, but He accepted people right where they were. We need to also learn to be real.

Matthew 11:19 The Son of Man came eating and drinking, and they say, 'Here is a glutton and a drunkard, a friend of tax collectors and "sinners."' But wisdom is proved right by her actions."

Matthew 9:12-13 On hearing this, Jesus said, "It is not the healthy who need a doctor, but the sick. But go and learn what this means: 'I desire mercy, not sacrifice.' For I have not come to call the righteous, but sinners."

Jesus was a friend of sinners; He was not afraid to get down on their level. Real friends can accept you the way you are because they are confident of whom they are.

[I] A friend **Imparts** Truth:

Jesus would not just leave an individual where they were; Jesus spoke the truth in love.

Real friends can accept you the way you are, but they won't leave you where you are. Jesus isn't afraid to get into our pig pens, but He comes there to lead us out of it.

Matthew 4:17 From that time on Jesus began to preach, "Repent, for the kingdom of heaven is near."

Proverbs 27:6 Wounds from a friend can be trusted, but an enemy multiplies kisses.

Ephesians 4:15 Instead, speaking the truth in love, we will in all things grow up into him who is the Head, that is, Christ.

[E] A friend is **Embracing**:

Jesus did not keep His love to Himself; rather He reached out to people with loving touches.

Luke 18:16 But Jesus called the children to him and said, "Let the little children come to me, and do not hinder them, for the kingdom of God belongs to such as these.

Luke 5:13 Jesus reached out his hand and touched the man [with leprosy]. "I am willing," he said. "Be clean!" And immediately the leprosy left him.

[N] A friend is **Not Selfish**:

Jesus put our need ahead of His comfort; we, too, need to learn to think of others first.

John 15:13 Greater love has no one than this that he lay down his life for his friends.

Romans 5:8 But God demonstrates his own love for us in this: While we were still sinners, Christ died for us.

[D] A friend is **Dedicated**:

Jesus did not give up on people; a real friend will stay beside you right through the very end.

Luke 23:34 Jesus said, "Father, forgive them, for they do not know what they are doing."

Jesus did not just say this for His enemies, who crucified Him; He also said it for His friends who had lost hope and run away. Jesus said it for you and me, for every time we turn from Him and fall into sin.

God created man in His image; God made man to share in relationship with one another. As we follow Jesus' example as the perfect friend, we can improve our relationships.

* * *

For some people when the honeymoon is over and weeks give way to months, which give way to years; the love that once burned with passion has more times than not become a weak flame. What happened? Where has the love gone? Many wish they could make the fire hotter; to make it like it first was at the start of the relationship.

There's a story about a woman who woke up and told her husband, "I just dreamed that you gave me a pearl necklace for Valentine's Day. What do you think it means?" Her husband responded: "You'll know tonight." That evening, the man came home with a small package and gave it to his wife. Delighted, she opened it to find... a book titled "*The Meaning of Dreams.*"

The fire usually goes out because we are not attending to it. With relationships that means we're out of touch—out of synch with our loves ones (as was the man in the story above). It does not have to be that way, though.

But sadly, today the dreams of repairing relationships can easily turn into nightmares at an alarming rate. George Barna, in his statistician reports, states "Baby Boomers are virtually certain to become the first generation for which a majority experience divorce."

* * *

One morning not long ago, I heard a tapping sound at intervals coming from across the street. I looked and saw a red bird trying to get into my neighbor's house by way of a window. He was looking for warmth. This cardinal sat on a tree branch, about four feet from the window and then suddenly flew right at the window hoping to get into the warm house. He smashed his head into the glass. You would think he learned his lesson. But no! That bird flew back to that branch, and four seconds later tried again, smash! With the same result. Not just once or twice but at least fifty times. Shaking my head I gave up watching him and turned away.

It is hard to grow a new way of life doing the same old things.

Many of us in long term loving relationships suffer because we insist on looking for something new and different while religiously practicing the same old things. When you do the same thing the same way and expect a different outcome you set yourself up for a letdown. The Bible talks about having a mind change: Let this mind be in you which is.... Be yet transformed by the renewing of your mind... Faith comes by hearing and hearing by the Word... all suggest change!

We all desire an innate loving relationship. We all want friendships that speak to our needs, but our needs are not the only needs in a relationship.

It's one thing to have a relationship but it's quite another to keep one going successfully. It requires a willingness to change! Give! Grow!

The question: What can be done to make our relationships stronger, more fulfilling, and whole?

How can you or I rekindle for example, the flame in our marriages, or to experience the feelings of love? How do we get to the point of giving and receiving love sufficiently? Well, a loving atmosphere must be created and maintained—a mutual understanding of love is required.

To understand love, one needs to go to the book of love. And there is no other book that defines love better than the Bible. It provides the answer to our conditions. Scripture is full of rich insights for relationship building and there is none better than Paul's letter to the church at Philippi. Paul wrote this "love letter" to the congregation who he knew was struggling specifically in the area of unity. You cannot have a strong relationship without a real unity of purpose. If there is no unity there will be no clear understanding (and feeling) of love. I repeat: Starting a relationship is the easy part, keeping it whole requires the ability to produce and maintain unity.

So how do we build unity in our relationships? How do we rekindle the dreams of a strong relationship and connection with others?

Paul provides several realistic principles we can employ daily.

First Principle: we need to encourage one another.

Everyone wants and needs to be encouraged. When was the last time you praised your significant other with reassuring words? Everyone needs to feel good about their self. And no one can encourage you more than the one closest to you. We tend to feel our own sufferings and forget about the hurts of those close to us. Life is difficult enough. And the one you live with can make your life one of peace or should you ignore them... make your life feel empty and unappreciated.

We all need inspiration, a pat on the back, a boost in our daily lives. Remember, give and you shall receive.

George M. Adams rightly comments there are high spots in all of our lives and most of them have come through encouragement from someone else. I don't care how great, how famous, or how successful a man or woman may be; each hungers for approval, applause and inspiration. While we don't want to become prideful from insincere praise, we should accept meaningful praise.

Actor, Jimmy Stewart stayed young until the day he died at age eighty-nine. Although extraordinarily talented, he remained touched by the fact that he was a celebrity. One time a stranger put his hand out and said, "Mr. Stewart, I don't guess it means much to you, but I want you to know I think you're wonderful." Taking the man's hand to shake it, Jimmy held on to it tightly, looked him in the eye, and said, "It means everything to me." He understood how important praise was.

Paul started his all-important letter with a word of encouragement and the central theme of his encouragement was Christ!

There is nothing more important than to have Christ as the center of your inspiration. Looking at what He has done for us should encourage and help us to inspire someone else. He says, "I will never leave you or forsake you!"

We have to feel, "I can lift you because he is lifting me." The more time I spend with Him the higher the quality of time I have to spend with others. He loves you just as you are and He can handle the real you. Christ loves us into change. He encourages us into becoming better and He stays right there with us through the struggles. We all need to know there's somebody lifting us up so we can lift others!

Second Principle: We must comfort one another.

Because of the "comfort from Jesus's love" Paul had affection for the congregation at Philippi. The same applies to any relationship. Any comfort you or I give in Christ will grow affection in our relationships, including our intimate relationships.

When we sincerely comfort someone it is more than likely that they will value and appreciate you. To do it without expectation often results in the positive connection that is most important in our lives.

One the reasons people may love but not like each other is because there tends to be little in the way of comforting and appreciation shown in ways small and large. Many people have no problem consoling those outside their home or relationship but find it difficult to do so for the one they share their life with!

Everyone is going through something... and sometimes it is signaled in hard to discern ways (especially if the person is uncomfortable with displaying or talking about how they feel). By understanding that is so, we can become more aware of what is going on with those who mean the most to us. A good relationship requires diligence and it requires doing the little things that prevent relationships from splintering and people from drifting apart.

Third Principle: Spending time with one another.

"Fellowship with the Spirit" was what Paul and the Philippians experienced together, with the understanding that the Holy Spirit helps believers cope with one another in their weakness. And the Spirit helps us in our weakness.

An important and often unasked question is, "You can love me not only when all is well but can you handle loving me when things are messed or going wrong?

Understand this—it's very important—we must look at and love ourselves first so we can love others the way they should be loved. We all must realize and acknowledge that we had to come from and through difficulties, too. Doing that self-assessment humanizes our thoughts and puts into context what's going on with other people in their lives. It enables us to feel for them because we have perspective.

So if each believer is helped in his or her weakness, then it is not so difficult to help and love others through their weaknesses. That is a key component that keeps people and relationships together!

But simply spending time without fellowship is wasted time. This is where the concept of being equally yoked come into play. If your choice for a relationship is someone that you have nothing in common with other than an attraction; then there will be a problem long term if there is no fellowship or unity of the spirit.

Reassurance will develop the relationship to a certain level but issues will develop over time without true fellowship. Being on the same page and working towards the same goal create critical bonds that make a relationship strong enough to work through any challenges or difficulties.

We have fellowship because we are yoked together in our struggles and in our victories, in our pressures and in our praise. We have fellowship as we spend time believing in the same things, trusting in the same God and living a life together that glorifies His ability to do abundantly above all that we can hope, dream or think.

Fourth Principle: Be tender and compassionate to one another.

What is tenderness and compassion? The words refer to what's inside us—literally. The Jews saw our inner parts as the source of the more tender affections—feelings. Compassion was literally the movement of the intestines.

In Paul's case, it was the affectionate feelings Paul had for the Philippians congregation and they for him.

Interestingly enough, tenderness and compassion we feel for our self will always show itself outwardly in acts of kindness and caring for others. We should see others as an extension of ourselves. When they do well we feel well, when they are happy we are happy, when they succeed we are part of their success.

Being kind is so important in strengthening the light of love in any relationship. Telling me you love me is one thing but what you do to show me is what ultimately matters.

Family

Warren Buffet is one of the richest men in the world. And it is interesting to note Buffet is one of only a few who acquired wealth through investing. I am sure it is no surprise that many investors look to him for advice. His firm, Berkshire Hathaway, has one of the most widely read annual reports issued and books have been written about his investment strategies. If you could sit down with Warren Buffet for a while and get some investment tips I'm sure you would. Am I right about that?

Investments are usually thought of as being made in companies, in real estate or perhaps even in commodities (like gold or oil, etc.). When it comes to companies, the kind that Warren Buffet invests in; the greatest asset is its people. In business, its people, the personnel that make the business operate, are often referred to as "human capital." Without people a business cannot exist, it cannot operate and it cannot make money—the very thing that investors require in exchange for their investment.

Relationships are investments and no investment is more valuable to us over the course of our life than family—that is truly the human capital most important to us.

And if you could get some investment tips on how to grow the quality of your human capital interactions I'm sure you would be interested. Am I right about that?

Well, if you pick up your Bible you will find in it a treasure of investment strategies for growing family relationships. It contains countless pro-family pro-human capital principles and precepts. If we learn and practice them they will make our families and relationships immensely valuable and that is the measure of true wealth.

I'll share with you here some of the knowledge found in the text:

Tip #1: Understanding

The first important principle in building wealth in our relationships, especially in our family interactions, is to understand each other.

How many of you own a smartphone, iPod, iPad or other computer or entertainment system?

Probably quite a few of you.

How many of you know how to program it?

Probably not very many.

There is a big difference between owning something and understanding how it works.

Those devices, created to be reasonably simple to use, are complex and sophisticated devices that require specific knowledge (and ability to apply it) in order to program.

Families are simple to be part of, but because humans can be inherently complex systems in and of themselves, they can often be hard to make run smoothly for long periods of time. People who have a nodding acquaintance with a second language know the gap between hearing words and understanding the meaning of those words. Because humans are driven by emotions and intellect... that can make for problems when trying to understand each other. And that does not happen without effort—it's not a casual happenstance.

Husbands are directly instructed to understand their wives. Now, I know some husbands who would say that it would be easier to understand quantum physics. And guys, I know some wives who would say the same thing about us!

In Peter 3:7 it states, "You husbands likewise, live with your wives in an understanding way, as with a weaker vessel, since she is a woman; and grant her honor as a fellow heir of the grace of life, so that your prayers may not be hindered." (NASB)

Now while the text is directly addressed to husbands it is not bad biblical interpretation to suggest that the principle of understanding one another can be applied to other relationships as well.

What does it mean to understand another person? It means to "make what is important to the other person as important to you as the other person is to you."

For instance, I recall one father who was not much of a sports fan but had a son who developed an interest in hockey. So one year he took his son to as many hockey games as he could. It cost him some money and time, but proved to be a strong bonding experience for them. One of his friends asked him in the midst of the hockey season, "Do you like hockey that much?" He said, "No, but I like my son that much!"

How do we develop such an understanding spirit?

By making the time to really get to know each other and that largely comes from making a point of listening to each other. I believe it was Yogi Berra who said, "You can hear an awful lot by just listening."

James 1:19 states, "That we should be 'quick to listen, slow to speak and slow to become angry.'" (NLT)

I don't know of any child or husband or wife that would be repulsed by a parent or spouse who was quick to really listen to them.

Tip #2: Keep commitments

It has been said we should be "generous with praise, but cautious with promises."

Parents, we need to do everything we can to keep promises we make to our children. Spouses, we need to do everything we can to keep our promises to each other. Children you need to do everything you can to keep your promises to your parents.

Why is keeping our commitments and honoring our promises so important? Because we all tend to construct our hopes around promises.

When a man promises to love a woman until death they do part, that gives the woman security to become all she was meant to be in the marriage relationship.

Ecclesiastes 5:4-5 says, "When you make a promise to God, don't delay in following through, for God takes no pleasure in fools." Keep all the promises you make to him. It is better to say nothing than to promise something that you don't follow through on. (NLT)

We can infer from this text that same holds true in our commitments to others. In other words, we are to be loyal. Proverbs 3:3-4 says, "Never let loyalty and kindness get away from you! Wear them like a necklace; write them down within your heart. Then you will find favor with both God and people, and you will gain a good reputation." (NLT)

When we keep our commitments it builds trust. And there is no such thing as a healthy relationship apart from trust. Trust is the firm foundation upon which a family is built.

But keeping commitments can be costly. I remember one time when I was invited to a dinner meeting where the pastor of the largest Protestant church in America was going to be speaking. I really wanted to go, but when I looked at my calendar I saw that I had made a previous commitment to some students in our church. That was tough for me, but I felt my previous obligation was more important. I know some parents in this church who travel as a part of their profession. They will drive all night long in order to make it to a child's school program they promised they would be at. You can be assured when the child sees them, not only are they happy, but that parent has instilled within the child the importance of keeping commitments.

Husbands and wives, when was the last time we visited the vows (a.k.a., commitments) we made on our wedding day?

When we married we made a commitment that next to God our spouse would be the most important relationship in our lives.

Does our time and attention reflect that?

Tip #3: Give some respect

R.E.S.P.E.C.T. is not just something Aretha Franklin wanted; it is something all of us in any relationship want. In fact it is next to impossible to have a deep relationship with another person when there is no respect.

Could it be the reason some of us are not experiencing the kind of relationship God wants to have because we do not have respect for him? And could it be that the reason some family relationships are not secure is because God is not respected? Proverbs 14:26 states, "Those who fear (or respect) the Lord are secure; he will be a place of refuge for their children." (NLT)

Another word for respect is "honor." Romans 12:10 states that as Christ followers we are to take delight in honoring each other.

Did you catch that?

We are to "delight" in honoring another person. It is not supposed to be a hassle or something to dread. When we delight in honoring another person it boosts their feeling of value.

How can we show that we are honoring the people in our family relationships?

- By respecting each other's property

- By respecting each other's privacy
- By respecting each other's time

The people who have the most difficulty respecting others are those with an inflated idea of their own importance; the sinfully proud. Philippians 2:3 tells us to be humble, thinking of others as better than you. Don't think only about your own affairs, but be interested in others, too, and what they are doing. (NLT)

Tip #4: Offer encouragement

Perhaps the easiest way to grow a healthy relationship is to offer encouragement. A well-known actress once said, "We live by encouragement, we die without it... slowly, sadly and angrily."

Thessalonians 5:11 says, "Therefore encourage one another and build each other up, just as in fact you are doing." (NIV)

How can we encourage one another in our homes?

By smiling (is one way).

Job, a man acquainted with grief and sorrow, in the chapter 29 of the book that bears his name, was recalling the days before he was visited with calamity. He said that when people around him were discouraged, I smiled at them. My look of approval was precious to them. (NLT)

Never underestimate the power of a smile. A smile not only increases your face value, but it warms the heart of those you give it to.

By our words.

Someone noted, "Man doesn't live by bread alone. He also needs buttering up." Words are power in that they can do enormous harm and amazing good.

By pointing out the positive.

A reporter once asked Andrew Carnegie, the great entrepreneur of an earlier generation, why he hired 43 millionaires to work for him. Carnegie pointed out that those men were not millionaires when he hired them.

The reporter then asked, "How did you develop these men to become so valuable to you that you paid them so much money?"

Carnegie replied that people are developed the same way gold is mined. When gold is mined, several tons of dirt must be moved to get an ounce of gold; but you don't go into the mine looking for dirt—you go in looking for gold!

Start today to look for gold in your child, in your spouse and in your parents. Jesus certainly must have seen the gold in the disciples he chose.

By giving gifts.

Are there any Barnabas' in your house?

In Acts 4:36-37 we read about a man named Joseph; the one the apostles nicknamed Barnabas, which means "Son of Encouragement." He was from the tribe of Levi and came from the island of Cyprus. He sold a field he owned and brought the money to the apostles for those in need. (NLT). One of the ways he practiced encouragement was by giving gifts.

Tip #5: Ask for and offer forgiveness

I saved this best tip for last.

Anyone who lives in a family of any kind knows that people will disappoint and hurt you. I asked my mom and dad, who've been married for 54 years, what were the secrets to their long and happy marriage. One gem of wisdom was, "You overlook a lot of little things and you forgive each other."

Colossians 3:13 states, Bear with each other and forgive whatever grievances you may have against one another. Forgive as the Lord forgave you.

But forgiveness is not natural. It seems to be normal to carry a grudge; to record all wrongs in read on a legal pad in our minds; to think of ways of getting back at those who hurt us.

Yet the Bible is clear in its instruction. As we have experienced forgiveness from God we are to forgive others.

The Spanish have a story about a father and son who became estranged.

The son left home, and the father later set out to find him. He searched for months with no success. Finally, in desperation, the father turned to the newspaper for help. His ad simply read, "Dear Paco, meet me in front of this newspaper office at noon on Saturday. All is forgiven. I love you. Your father."

On Saturday, eight hundred young men named Paco showed up looking for forgiveness and love from their estranged fathers.

Families today are filled with people who desperately long for reconciliation.

Some of you need to experience that kind of forgiveness from God.

Forgiveness for yourself and forgiveness for others.

* * *

All of what we discussed in this chapter, if applied, will not only show you that you are not alone, but will also let you create valuable relationships (physically and spiritually) that are the true wealth and sustenance of our lives.

If you have a family and or good friends, focus on strengthening your relationship with them. And it's not only about talking with them; it's about doing things together, it's about shared experiences (both work and play). These are the common glue that binds the fabric of our lives with those we love and need the most.

If you don't have a family; look to those that can be a surrogate—your church, another organization or again, your friends. Where you can interact on a regular basis with them and develop bonds of appreciation and respect.

Becoming more engaged and active with others is an important part of finding your own way; to finding your purpose as it relates to the larger picture of your life.

No Man is an island,
Entire of itself.
Each is a piece of the continent,
A part of the main.
If a clod be washed away by the sea,
Europe is the less.
As well as if a promontory were.
As well as if a manor of thine own
Or of thine friend's were.
Each man's death diminishes me,
For I am involved in mankind.
Therefore, send not to know
For whom the bell tolls,
It tolls for thee.

-John Donne

Chapter 3

The Turning Point

"Begin living life instead of letting life live you..."

-Dennis Lowery

There are many key points in life. The important thing, and what you must do, is to identify the critical ones that lead to self-realization, self-determination and self-actualization. These, in the aggregate, form your purpose.

Author Dennis Lowery, in writing and talking about leading a self-determined life, uses what he calls, "The oxygen mask analogy;" with his permission I'm sharing it with you:

At the front of the aircraft a flight attendant stands drawing your attention to the safety instructions for your flight. She gestures and points to the exits for the aircraft in the event of an emergency and then describes what will happen if the aircraft cabin should become depressurized.

"Oxygen and the air pressure are always being monitored. In the event of a decompression, an oxygen mask will automatically drop down in front of you. To start the flow of oxygen, pull the mask towards you. Place it firmly over your nose and mouth, secure the

elastic band behind your head, and breathe normally. Although the bag does not inflate, oxygen is flowing to the mask. If you are travelling with a child or someone who requires assistance, secure your mask first, and then assist the other person. Keep your mask on until a uniformed crew member advises you to remove it."

If you are someone who flies frequently, possibly you don't pay a lot of attention to the announcement. But within it are two statements that are particularly important when it comes to you and your life:

"Oxygen and the air pressure are always being monitored" and *"secure your mask first, and then assist the other person."*

The first statement cites the important fact that two critical things are being watched. From a personal standpoint I take monitoring to mean awareness and true self-awareness requires total honesty. Honesty about who we really are inside and what we really want.

The second statement is clear. The most important thing to do first is to take care of you.

This is critical and absolutely essential to success and happiness in life.

If you do not take care of yourself... if you do not focus on yourself first... then it is impossible for you to be of value to anyone else.

That's not being selfish; it's being realistic. That pragmatic viewpoint does not mean respecting yourself requires demeaning or devaluing others. For people to appreciate us we must first appreciate ourselves (yes, with all our flaws... "warts and blemishes" both figuratively and literally... we have to feel good deep inside about who we are).

The world doesn't need martyrs or those who always see themselves as a victim and I'd certainly bet that your friends and your family (the people who care most about you) don't need you to be either one. And if they do then they fall under the category of a type of person(s) you need to separate yourself from. If anything or anyone in life requires you to be a martyr or victim, you have to question their level of respect and or love for you or its validity. You don't have to live that kind of life.

I believe God, in all names and manifestations, wants us to be happy and happiness really starts with yourself. Knowing who you are, what you want and having self-respect.

So put your oxygen mask on first.

* * *

World-renowned writer and author, Paulo Coelho, in his international bestseller, *The Alchemist*, tells of the world's greatest lie:

"At a certain point in our lives, we lose control of what's happening to us, and our lives become controlled by fate."

He's right.

That is the world's biggest lie and one that many people have let eat into their soul to such a degree that they have completely abrogated their right to take life in their own hands. They have either forgotten or never worked to find the one thing that refutes the world's biggest lie.

There is an often quoted piece of scripture, in the Bible, that is very important in realizing how to bring about your own turning point: Romans 8:28 says, "And we know that all things work together for good, for those who love God, who are called according to his purpose." While many people, both religious and not, refer to this (or the gist of it); there is often a disconnect between quoting such words of affirmation and actually living them daily.

"Purpose" is the relevant word when it comes to proving that lie wrong. Purpose will drive us (you and me) to have control of our life and if you lack it—and know its absence—you can discover it. But only if you work at it and realize your turning point can only come once you have determined what your purpose is. Following your purpose is something you must do every day... or it (and what you want or desire) can slip away from you.

If we are dissatisfied with something specific about ourselves or perhaps just in general are discontented with our lives; at some point we must come to the conclusion that, *"enough is enough"* and make a change. You cannot bring about improvement in your life if you keep doing (and thinking) the same things day in and day out.

We all have potential. We each have some level of talent, skills, knowledge and a uniqueness that makes us who we are. But the extent to which we reach beyond any real or perceived limitations and restrictions placed on us (by social standards, family, economics or stifling acculturated political practices) is largely based on our willingness to face our self. The "you" that existed and spoke with the boldness of a child before the reality of adulthood took over and quieted your voice. Or the "you" that lives inside but you've never been able to show or reveal to the world.

Few are able to find their way back to the true "you" while coping with the struggles of being what you are to others. We are all something to someone else. We are fathers, mothers, family members, a support system, an enabler in some cases, and much more to and for others. Being those things may be good or not so good—some are a pleasurable responsibility, the ones that you relish and look forward to and others can be the heaviest burden to carry. And some are hybrids: at times a worthwhile task or duty and at other times the bitterest of efforts to take on and perform on a daily basis. It is in dealing with the daily grind that we lose ourselves. Each day is layer upon layer that stifles and ultimately deadens the soul within. And it can't free itself on its own.

To find our self again, to realize that the soul inside us still has a spark of light, is a process of discovery. There needs to be a time and place when you can work at peeling away the layers. No matter whom you are; in spite of the fame, popularity, boredom, despair, isolationism, busyness, and uncertainty there must be dedicated time for self-awareness. Time to ask, "Who am I at this moment? Who is it I hope to be in the future? Tomorrow? Next week... next month... next year? Am I working towards becoming who I want to become? Am I planting the appropriate seeds that will come to fruition in the way that I hope and dream of?"

A critical turning point in our lives is created when we've peeled away enough to realize we are falling short of what we want (or need) and that what we are currently doing (or not doing) has a direct impact on whether we succeed or fail.

To hit a target you must do two things: 1) identify the target, then 2) aim and fire with skill.

What is the goal or objective I am reaching towards and why? Has it changed and will it possibly change again? When you can define exactly what that target is... you can become focused on evaluating and assessing the situation. That will tell you whether or not you have a chance at hitting the target. Is it too far away? Do I currently have the right means to hit the target?

Let's assume that target is to rediscover "you" so that it becomes the turning point to go from what was, to what is, to what might be and to what you want to happen. Target identified.

What am I reading, listening to or engaged in, that will aid me in becoming the real me (or the me I want to become) or that will prevent me? Without becoming too philosophical, it is an absolute truth that we become who we are through our experiences, whether those experiences are planned or unplanned. So plan what you do going forward. Create the experiences that will help you reach your objective and become the means by which you hit your target.

What do you see around you?

When you look at the people around you what do you see? Do you see impressive people, dressed in fine clothes that have it all together? Or do you see hurting people in need of comfort; troubled people in need of peace; sick people who need healing? Or both? Probably both at some point and quite a few in the middle of the two extremes.

Marshall Hayden wrote an article a few years ago entitled, *"Would Every Non-Hurter Please Stand Up?"* He pointed out that people come to church wearing their best clothes and with their best smiles. Everybody looks happy, so we assume everything is okay. But he suggests that we need to look beyond the facade and realize that the pews are full of hurting people.

The streets and homes are full of people who have the same or perhaps even more difficult challenges as you do. He wrote, "Over here is a family with an income of $550 a week and an outgo of $1,000. Over there is a family with two children who, according to their dad, are "failures." "You're stupid. You never do anything right," he is constantly telling them. The lady over there just found a tumor that tested positive. The Smith's little girl has a hole in her heart. Sam and Louise just had a nasty fight. Each is thinking of divorce. Last Monday Jim learned that he was being laid off. Sarah has tried her best to cover the bruises her drunken husband inflicted when he came home Friday night. That teen over there feels like he is on the rack, pulled in both directions. Parents and church pull one way; peers and glands pull the other.

Then there are those of us with lesser hurts, but they don't seem so small to us: a spouse who doesn't seem to care anymore, a boring job, a poor grade, a friend or parent who is unresponsive... on and on the stories go. The lonely, the dying, the discouraged, the exhausted, they're all here."

In the face of that, there is good news. Jesus said, "Come to me, all you who are weary and burdened and I will give you rest. Take my yoke upon you and learn from me, for I am gentle and humble in heart, and you will find rest for your souls" [Matthew 11:28-30].

63

This is not to say that He will heal every problem immediately if we just have enough faith. Jesus said clearly that we will have trouble in this world. But He can resolve life's serious problems if we trust in Him. In some cases, He may resolve the problem immediately, even miraculously. In others, He grants the power to endure the difficulty and triumph over it.

All of us... all the people we see (including that person in the mirror) either embrace or ignore turning points in their life. What we do when faced with them (whether they are of our own creation or circumstance) is what can affect our lives dramatically.

We have within us that which can create what we wish for ourselves. The uncertain person in that mirror can become the radiant portrait—that confident and secure person that we want to share with the world. It's in our hands.

The healing of the lame man at the pool of Bethesda, recorded in John 5:1-15, is a dramatic example of Jesus' wondrous power. Here was a man who had been unable to walk for 38 years. He had been a burden to people. He probably had little sense of self-worth. But Jesus had pity on him and healed him. And it's one of the few times the Scripture records Jesus healing someone when He was not asked to do so. Let's see how Jesus motivated this man to become a candidate for healing.

These same four prerequisites are necessary for us today and applicable whether you are religious or not:

1. HE IDENTIFIED WHAT HE WANTED

First of all, Jesus encouraged the man to identify what he wanted. "When Jesus saw him lying there and learned that he had been in this condition for a long time, He asked him, 'Do you want to get well?'" That sounds like an absurd question. Of course this man wanted to get well! You wouldn't ask a starving man, "Do you want food," would you?

Actually, it was a very valid question, for there are people who, if given an opportunity for healing, might actually choose to remain sick. If they are sick or seem incapable they're free of any unpleasant responsibilities, and they get sympathy.

They can manipulate people in that way to avoid many things, ranging from work to meaningful conversation. Or to punish them if they are internalizing guilt by emphasizing their illness or weakness, which ends up a physical manifestation—they make themselves sick or infirm.

Some people will do things to themselves unconsciously that hurt them. Some flawed people even embrace making themselves incapable or unworthy. Dave Reavor, a disabled Viet Nam veteran, tells of a young man in the 1960s who didn't want to be drafted. So he had all his teeth pulled out to make himself unfit for military duty. When he took his physical he was declared unfit because of flat feet!

So when Jesus asked, "Do you want to get well?" He seems to be saying, "You have friends who bring you here, and you've developed friendships with others who come here regularly. If I heal you, your life will do a complete reversal. You'll be expected to get a job and relate to people on a different basis. Are you ready for that change? Do you really want to get well?"

If your life is not what it should be; if you are not the person that you want to be; in order to begin to change there are questions you need to ask yourself—and to answer them honestly:

What do you want? The first step to gaining something is to want it specifically.

Are you willing to make changes, or do what is necessary, in order to get what you want?

If you want something you don't have that generally means you are not able to get it or do it... yet. You have to define what you need to do; what actions you need to take to make things happen.

Doctor's Minirth and Meyer have written a book about overcoming depression titled "*Happiness Is a Choice.*" They wrote, "As psychiatrists, we cringe whenever Christian patients use the words, `I can't' and `I've tried.' Any good psychiatrist knows that `I can't' and `I've tried' are merely lame excuses. We insist that our patients stop saying `can't' and say `won't' instead."

"They need to see what they are really doing, so we make them face up to it by saying, `I just won't get along with my wife.' `My husband and I won't communicate.' `I won't discipline my kids the way I should.' `I won't find time to pray.' `I won't stop gossiping.' When they change their "can'ts" to "won'ts" they stop avoiding the truth and start facing reality."

We need to face the truth of our lives and who we are squarely without trying to weasel out. We need to determine what we really want, and believe that we are capable of getting them. Even if it means making changes.

2. HE QUIT BLAMING OTHER PEOPLE

A second prerequisite for this man's healing was to quit blaming others for his problem.

There was a local belief that the waters of Bethesda had healing powers. Some Biblical manuscripts read that "An

angel of the Lord came down and stirred up the waters."
Earlier manuscripts did not contain that explanation, and
many scholars believe the stirring of the water was from
an underground spring that would occasionally experience
extreme pressure. Whatever caused the disturbance, the
people believed that when the waters of Bethesda bubbled
up, the first one in the water would be cured.

So when Jesus asked, "Do you want to get well?" the man
replied, "Sir, I have no one to help me into the pool when
the water is stirred. While I am trying to get in, someone
else goes down ahead of me" [John 5:7]. He was
complaining, "Every time the water bubbles up, no one is
here to help me into the pool. It's always the stronger ones
who reach the water first. It's a shame those of us who
need it the most get the least amount of help. It's been
that way for 38 years."

When God asked Adam why he disobeyed, Adam
explained, "The woman you gave me persuaded me to
eat."

When Moses asked his brother Aaron why he permitted
the Israelites to worship a golden calf, Aaron said, "The
people pressured me to do something since you were gone
so long, Moses. They wanted gods like the Canaanites. I
just threw their jewelry into the fire and out came the
calf." Blame the people, blame Moses for taking so long,
blame the Canaanites, blame the fire even! But don't
blame me!

When Pilate was forced to make a decision about Jesus, he said, "I wash my hands of this matter. Jesus is yours; do with Him as you please. But I'm innocent of this whole matter."

People do the same thing today.

It's so easy to blame other people for our problems. That has been Man's scapegoat from the beginning. And it's wrong and a major factor in failing to have the life that you want or to become the person that you want to be.

How often do we hear people say things like, "I'd stop drinking if my wife would quit nagging me!" "I'd work harder, but no one appreciates my effort." "I'd make better grades, but my teacher doesn't like me."

There are any number of excuses that can be made to not improve ourselves but very few real reasons. When you lay the fault on someone or something else you give them or it power over you.

How would that make you feel?

Not too good I suspect and if so... you should get mad at yourself. Mad just enough to decide that "enough is enough, I'm not going to accept this anymore."

* * *

King William of Potsdam once visited a prison in England. Every prisoner brought before him claimed to be innocent, and pleaded for a pardon except for one man who admitted his guilt. King William said to the warden, "Get this guilty man out of the prison before he corrupts all these innocent men!" And the man was set free.

We have such a difficult time saying, "I'm responsible." We blame heredity, environment, and circumstances; everything except ourselves. Yet what is most important to success and to find happiness in life is to accept responsibility for our own behavior.

Romans 14:12 says, "Each of us will give an account of himself to God." Heredity and environment play a part in influencing us, but we can rise above that if we want to. Some of the world's most successful people had terrible pasts. Some of the most privileged wind up being complete failures.

Maybe it's time to quit blaming mom and dad or an ex-spouse or a relative who abused you in some way, and say with the old spiritual, *"It's me, it's me, O Lord, standin' in the need of prayer. Not my brother, not my sister, but it's me, O Lord, standin' in the need of prayer."*

3. HE STRETCHED BEYOND HIMSELF

Jesus also motivated the lame man to stretch beyond himself. "Then Jesus said to him, `Get up! Pick up your mat and walk. At once the man picked up his mat and walked."

Jesus frequently required a dedicated effort on the part of a person requesting healing. Not always, but often, He required a response of faith before He would heal. He said to the 10 lepers, "Go show yourself to the priests," and as they went they were healed. He said to the man with a withered hand, "Stretch forth your hand." When the man made the effort, his hand was healed. Jesus put clay on the eyes of a blind man and said, "Go wash in the pool of Siloam." When he washed, he could see.

Jesus said to this man, "Pick up your mat and walk."

This was not a test of his faith in Jesus because the lame man didn't know who Jesus was. It was a test of his resolve, and of his willingness to make an effort to help himself. Jesus asked the man to attempt the one thing that he hadn't done for 38 years. When the man made the effort, he was healed at once.

Reaching and acting on a turning point in your life is a "miracle" not reserved for the religious or bestowed by God. It is the type of quiet sensation that happens daily to men and women. It's the "enough is enough" kicking them into gear and making them strive to be more... to do more. To take action to fulfill their wants.

For a turning point to have meaning we have to stretch beyond where we are at that point in time. If we want to make things different in or for ourselves, there must be effort.

4. HE GAVE CREDIT

After he was healed, the man was motivated to give testimony that Jesus had healed him. The day on which this took place was a Sabbath, and so the Jews said to the man who had been healed, "It is the Sabbath; the law forbids you to carry your mat." But he replied, "The man who made me well said to me, `Pick up your mat and walk.'"

So they asked him, "Who is this fellow who told you to pick it up and walk?" The man who was healed had no idea who it was, for Jesus had slipped away into the crowd.

Notice that when Jesus healed He didn't make a big production of it. He didn't put up banners to draw attention to Himself. He would say, "Don't tell anyone about this," or afterwards He would quietly leave, not needing any attention.

God doesn't need a circus to heal. If He chooses to, it's usually without fanfare. You don't need to talk loudly about what you're doing or planning to do. Just do it.

As you reach your turning point, and you take action and begin seeing positive results, don't blow your own horn. Keep focused on the task(s) at hand and be thankful for what you are accomplishing... and grateful for wherever the spark came from that is driving you to make positive changes to your life.

* * *

These four things are critical for you to reach your own turning point and just as importantly they are how to sustain progress once your turning point goads you into action.

Chapter 4

A Passport to a Better Tomorrow

"...the location of the body is much less important than the location of the mind, and the former has surprisingly little influence on the latter. The heart goes where the head takes it, and neither cares much about the whereabouts of the feet."

- John Tierney, New York Times

Everything. All that we are and that we become. Everything starts with how you think and what you believe.

And as the above quote suggests, how focused your thinking is, is tied to how happy you are. My own opinion is that you must generate a fair share of focused thought to have a meaningful life. And that a meaningful life is a happier one.

To have a significant life, we don't all have to be geniuses or scientists whose time is probably primarily spent in thought or contemplation.

We don't have to fixate on serious topics such as how to achieve peace in the Middle-East, how to fix our nations educational system, or in figuring out how some public figures of questionable intellect (and intent) manage to garner national attention when we need intelligent people in politics (in both parties). Quasi-Political-Media types that play to the attention and support of the mindless are not going to come up with solutions to the problems we face as a nation. All they do is take attention away from the serious work of resolving issues and solving problems.

Back to the subject though...

Daydreaming, idle speculation and stream-of-consciousness thinking are fine and everyone has those moments during the day. But consider this:

"Life is not long," Samuel Johnson said, **"and too much of it must not pass in idle deliberation how it shall be spent."**

I know that I am always happiest when I am focusing on something. When I have something definite that I am trying to give complete attention to—that is when I feel most alive. The focus improves the work and creates a strong feeling of accomplishment. And accomplishment at many different levels in life is something that that we should all desire and strive for.

To make our own lives better (and those around us) takes concentration on those things that are important to us. That and perseverance will pay off for you.

I believe that is where the heart and mind become one and is what I call finding your purpose!

Perhaps your life is not enough of one thing or too much of another or any combination things that has led you to the point where you've determined a purpose. You've reached your turning point. Now what?

In the busyness of our lives we sometimes overlook the common sense things we need to do for ourselves and others. We don't sit still long enough to give them the thought (and action) they deserve. One of the common sense things we must do is to forgive ourselves.

Forgiving yourself is not forgetting or attempting to erase the reality of your past actions and the results and circumstances of your life. We are all accountable for what we do (or don't do) in life. Forgiveness is acknowledging this and being strong enough to do what's right and move beyond the past to build a better life now and in the future.

We look back over our lives with perfect vision and see so much to blame ourselves for. We see so many things that we now face—the reality of what our lives have become. There's so much that we should've and could've done differently but we didn't. And we must understand that life can't move forward if it's constantly held back by the past. Recriminations are some of the heaviest baggage we will ever carry.

Guilt. To remove it you have to look inside yourself. There is one essential thing to understand about guilt. Every human being bears some form of guilt. No one is perfect. No one is pure. So look deeply at yourself and understand that you're not alone in this.

What you must have, starting today, to create a better tomorrow?

You need faith.

Faith to keep moving forward toward the goals or target you identified. Faith that by following the means to reach or hit the target you'll get what you want. Faith that with that accomplishment you or your life will be better.

It has been said "Optimism is man's passport to a better tomorrow."

And I agree with that.

If provided with the appropriate mindset, tools, strategies, networks, and support for success, human beings have the right to be (and hopefully are) optimistic. These realties do not only improve opportunities for the individual but if practiced consistently and expertly can improve, restore and revitalize not only the individual but also communities. I believe if you improve the person—you improve what surrounds them through their empowerment and belief in the ability to manifest positive change. So while this book is about the individual; it's important here to talk about the bigger picture because while a community is made up of individuals—building a stronger community, in turn, helps to strengthen and provide opportunities for individuals within the community.

* * *

"A single event can awaken within us a stranger totally unknown to us. To live is to be slowly born."

-Antoine de Saint-Exupéry

Humans are creature of habit; we are most comfortable with what we are most familiar. When we are exposed to success regularly we begin to practice success. Even those who become exposed to positive experiences later in their young adult lives have a better chance at success.

Success breeds success.

Mentoring, mimicking, and practicing tenets that create opportunities for success requires exposure to successful individuals. Often that doesn't happen and there are circles of opportunity for which few are afforded entry.

Many disadvantaged groups suffer not because they are inherently predisposed to socioeconomic failure but because they are disconnected or disassociated from the well-organized practices of successful tight-knit groups and individuals. Breaking into positive networks, closed-door meetings, "invitation-only" social events and deciphering the code language of the successful is no small task especially when the interaction is limited or even worse not attempted because of a lack of faith that things can change for the better. They can.

Revitalizing a community requires buy-in, outside support and a realistic set of goals in proportion with existing resources—every community has them no matter how spare they may seem. And there are untapped resources as well. To find and effectively tie together these resources a sense of "team" leadership is required. Making an appropriate assessment of the community stake holders and strategies for valuing diversity in leadership, gaining an appreciation for historic leadership and understanding emerging leaders, are all vital steps towards reconciling tapped and untapped resources—and their effective use.

Many prosperous communities understand well the reality: When you "come up" you pull others up around you. That's the conversation we need to have so that very act can take place. To show how each of us as individuals have within the seeds of positive change to help our communities blossom and become that fertile ground to both live, raise children and thrive.

Changing your Mental Zip Code.

Elevating a person or community's consciousness requires a mental zip code change.

People can only do what they know. Leaders can only expect from those they lead the skill they have been given, taught or exposed to.

In the U.S. depending on your zip code you may be exposed to a more expansive, in-depth and better-tailored learning environment. Because everyone may not be able to afford to live in such a zip code you have to come up with realistic and meaningful strategies that speak to the equitable standardization of quality learning. That sets the foundation for an emotional, educational and ultimately economic zip code change without having to make a physical move now.

The notion of voice (your voice) comes from an internal sense of self-worth; it comes from having a true understanding of how valuable you are. And it is this "voice" that establishes that mental shift to take you to the "good" zip code.

But value, for many, comes from perception.

Many understand this but there are those that don't grasp the concept. *"Gold is gold and greed is good,"* they think and believe. But there comes a time when intrinsic value is far greater; when what's inside is so much more important than the trappings you see and the brocade that glitters and drapes just the right way. It's who and what you are inside that establishes your worth. The Reverend Albert E. Sims tells a story about this:

> A costly Diamond that had once sparkled in a lady's ring lay in a field amid tall grasses and oxeye daisies.
>
> Just above it, was a big Dewdrop that clung timidly to a nodding leaf.
>
> Overhead, the blazing sun shone in all his noonday glory.
>
> Ever since the first pink blush of dawn, the modest Dewdrop had gazed fixedly down upon the rich gem, but feared to address a person of such exalted consequence.

At last, a large Beetle, during his rambles, chanced to espy the Diamond, and he also recognized him to be someone of great rank and importance.

"Sire," he said, making a low bow, "permit your humble servant to offer you greeting."

"Tha—nks," responded the Diamond in languid tones of affectation.

As the Beetle raised his head from his profound bow, his gaze happened to alight upon the Dewdrop.

"A relative of yours, I presume, Sire?" he remarked affably, waving one of his feelers in the direction of the Dewdrop.

The Diamond burst into a rude, contemptuous laugh.

"Quite too absurd, I declare!" he exclaimed loftily.

"But there, what can you expect from a low, groveling beetle? Away, sir, pass on! Your very presence is distasteful to me. The idea of placing ME upon the same level—in the same family, as a low-born, mean, insignificant, utterly valueless——" Here the Diamond fairly choked for breath.

"But has he not beauty exactly like your own, Sire?" the Beetle ventured to interpose, though with a very nervous air.

"BEAU—TY!" flashed the Diamond, with fine disdain—"the impudent fellow merely apes and imitates ME. However, it is some small consolation to remember that 'Imitation is the sincerest flattery.' But, even allowing him to possess it, mere beauty without rank is ridiculous and worthless. A Boat without water—a Carriage, but no horses—a Well, but never a winch: such is beauty without rank and wealth! There is no real worth apart from rank and wealth. Combine Beauty, Rank, and Wealth, and you have the whole world at your feet. Now you know the secret of the world worshipping ME."

And the Diamond sparkled and gleamed with vivid, violet flashes, so that the Beetle was glad to shade his eyes.

The poor Dewdrop had listened silently to all that had passed, and felt so wounded, that at last he wished he never had been born. Slowly a bright tear fell and splashed the dust.

Just then, a Skylark fluttered to the ground and eagerly darted his beak at the Diamond.

"Alas!" he piped, with a great sob of disappointment. "What I thought to be a precious dewdrop is only a worthless diamond. My throat is parched for want of water. I must die of thirst!"

"Really? The world will never get over your loss," sneered the Diamond.

But a sudden and noble resolve came to the Dewdrop. Deeply did he repent his foolish wish. He could now lay down his life that the life of another might be saved!

"May I help you, please?" he gently asked.

The Lark raised his drooping head.

"Oh, my precious, precious friend, if you will, you can save my life!"

"Open your mouth then."

And the Dewdrop slid from the blade of grass, tumbled into the parched beak, and was eagerly swallowed.

"Ah—well, well!" pondered the Beetle as he continued his homeward way. "I've been taught a lesson that I shall not easily forget. Yes, yes!

Simple worth is far better than rank or wealth without modesty and unselfishness—and there is no true beauty where these virtues are absent!"

To speak and contribute your thoughts requires one to first believe he or she has something worth sharing and it will be heard in an environment of respect and receptivity. And perhaps most importantly... a level of reciprocity will occur and equally important is sustained.

When I talk about the importance of self; the importance of "Me"; I'm not saying we need to be self-centered or self-absorbed.

We don't need to become egotistical, arrogant or conceited—full of self-importance.

What I'm saying is that if you don't respect yourself then how in the world can you expect others to respect you. So self-worth is really self-appreciation and the realization that while you have flaws, as all humans do; you also have positive things that you make you worthwhile—there is value that you bring and by your character and actions you are deserving of respect. That is the foundation of your personal voice.

To help those around us to find their "voice" requires leadership. And the most effective leadership is perpetual. It's consistent and congruent. Effective leaders build leadership in others. From a community standpoint this is integral to help people discover that voice needed to bring about positive change to their life. This is especially true if the mission, vision and philosophy is to live beyond the leader's own existence.

The difference between being rich and being wealthy is wealth is self-perpetuating—being rich is not. Wealth continues to grow beyond the initial investment and as the investment grows those connected to the investment also grows. A rich person who does not understand this concept will soon find they are no longer rich. And so it goes with leadership.

An effective leader grows those tied to and invested in them and will benefit from the reputation, connections, associations, and mission generated and maintained by the interactions and adherence to a common purpose. As long as there is a connection to the mission of the leader the leader and the mission lives. If there is not—then the leader will soon find there is no one left to lead.

One of the greatest failings of any endeavor is the lack of support. Good leadership becomes great leadership when meaningful strategies to mentor, develop, and perpetuate the mission and vision in others presents all involved the potential for greatness that is then realized. It has been said no man is an island unto himself. Without support and a mindset that allows for an investment in others as well as a willingness to develop and trust others to lead, the vision dies and the leader is nullified. And so the opportunities for new voices to develop are quenched.

There needs to be a conscious effort in every community to build an environment that invites support for the leader. That engenders support for the vision and ultimately the leadership mission. Solidarity and strength of purpose in this gives confidence in what you are doing and this in turn trips a switch in your thinking—that all things are possible for you... and for your community.

Fragmented communities or those that possess the potential for effective leadership but have been denied the opportunity due to existing social-economic factors have to decide they need leadership—and failure is not an option. They must focus on specific areas that both invite diverse perspectives yet allows for consensus building. That is necessary to build an environment that meshes diverging interest and promotes collaboration. Bringing people together is in many ways is an art; it takes great patience and practice. It is important to establish operating ground rules at the start of any cooperative leadership initiative. Several key practices, proceedings and areas of focus in which all participants must agree to adhere to are essential for forward movement and to avoid contention during critical moments down the road.

Now we're back to the element that you need to initiate and sustain that forward movement. The progress necessary to create a better tomorrow for you and your community.

Faith.

How to grow your faith.

Think about these things that seemed difficult (and maybe even a bit scary) at first: learning to swim, learning how to ride a bike, learning how to skate, and learning how to drive or do anything that seemed complex or hard. They all started with the belief that we could do it. Yes, it might have been a bit shaky... kind of tenuous at first. But you stuck with it, then could do it reasonably well and maybe even became quite proficient. Doing it without conscious thought—accepting that the skill is inside you—just knowing what to do, when and how to do it as you went along. Faith is like that, too.

Believe that your faith can grow!

Remember when Jesus was in the boat and a great storm arose and the disciples woke Him because they were afraid? He looked at them and said, "O ye of little faith." Remember the lady whose daughter was possessed and she came and asked Jesus to touch her? As she persisted, Jesus finally looked at her and said, "Your faith is great!" Remember when Paul wrote to the church at Thessalonica? He said he was thankful because their faith was greatly enlarged."

Did you see the progression? Little—Great—Greatly Enlarged! If our faith is to expand, we must believe that it can!

A second way to have a powerful faith is to associate with others who have great faith.

Rom. 1:12: "That I may be encouraged together with you while among you, each of us by the other's faith, both yours and mine."

I Thess. 3:2: "...and we sent Timothy, our brother and God's fellow worker in the gospel of Christ, to strengthen and encourage you as to your faith."

Often good circumstances and bad friends equal problems. On the other hand, bad circumstances and good friends equal victory! People we associate with are like elevator buttons—they can take you up or down!

My faith has been enlarged to a great extent by the example of others—observing how they handled adversity and the challenges that life brings. It rubs off, this thing we call faith. The more we associate with those who really have faith in themselves, faith in doing what's right and faith in something larger than themselves, the more we will become a person of faith.

Can you think of someone whose faith has inspired you?

The life of D.L. Moody has been a constant encouragement to me. One time he said, "I prayed for faith and thought that someday it would come down and strike me like lightning. But faith didn't seem to come. One day I read in Romans that "faith comes by hearing and hearing by the word of God." I had up to this time, closed my Bible and prayed for faith. Now I opened my Bible and began to study and faith has been growing ever since."

The first morning I heard the mockingbird practicing his bag full of imitations outside my window, I was thrilled by the beauty of his songs. Gradually, however, I began to take this early morning songster for granted. One day as I awoke, it dawned on me that I no longer appreciated my regular visitor. It wasn't the mockingbird's fault. He was still there. His beautiful song hadn't changed, but I was no longer listening for it. As believers in Christ, we may have a similar experience hearing God speak to us in His Word.

When we are first saved, the Scriptures, with their soul-stirring instruction and vital spiritual food, are deeply satisfying. As time goes on, however, we routinely read those same portions over and over in a manner that no longer speaks to us.

Our spiritual senses grow dull and lethargic, and God's exhilarating Word becomes commonplace to us. But then, what joy we feel when a passage reveals an exciting truth, and once again we "hear" the Lord! Our faith in many things is like that, too. Do not take each day for granted and say, "today is just another day." Each day you need to fire your spirit up so that you can make your life incrementally better than the day before.

Remember the man in Matthew 17 who came to the disciples and asked them for help for his demon-possessed boy? He asked the disciples to pray for him. They prayed and nothing happened. Then Jesus prayed and something did happen—a miracle! The disciples got discouraged and said, "Lord, why is it when we prayed for him that nothing happened?" And the Lord answered, "It was because of your little faith." Then He talked to them about faith being the size of a mustard seed and how much growth potential it had. Referring to the boy who was possessed, Jesus said, "This kind does not go out except by prayer and fasting." In other words, there are some problems which are so huge that we must be totally immersed in prayer and fasting—believing God to give that for which we pray. Great problems demand great faith!

Dr. A.C. Dixon, a well-known pastor in Boston, found his church needed $5,000 to square accounts. He and his deacons prayed about it. One deacon rose and said, "Brethren, God has answered our prayers. He will send the money in next Sunday's collection. That Sunday it rained all day and the congregation was small. A deacon suggested that they not take the collection. But the deacon who had believed for a good offering said, "I didn't trust the weather; I trusted God!" They took the offering and it came to $5,600!"

Faith can be your most powerful ally and support as you change your life for the better.

Mark 9:23: "All things are possible to him that believes." Hebrews 11:1: "Faith gives substance to our hopes and makes us certain of realities we do not see." And then, of course, there are the many epigrams that abound today regarding faith:

"Faith sees the invisible, believes the incredible and receives the impossible."

"A little faith will bring your soul to heaven; a great faith will bring heaven to your soul."

"Faith, like muscle, grows strong with exercise."

There is a verse in the Bible that cites, "faith to faith" as key.

The first faith speaks of that which is primary (saving faith); the second faith is power-giving (fruitfulness). We build on the first faith (it is foundational); the second one identifies us.

The first faith is all about assurance; the second tells us what we can become. The first faith deals with redemption; the second deals with risk.

The first faith is a gift; the second is all about growth. But there is a complement to faith that is needed as well.

You need commitment.

Without it you (and anyone) will fail. Commitment is the determination to take what steps are necessary, guided by faith (in all we defined above), day in and day out. Commitment also means perseverance. Life is not easy. Changing your life is not easy.

But faith and commitment create hope... and if you hold them close to you and do each and every day what they require of you. Then you will begin to see that there is a brighter day coming. Your goals can be achieved and dreams realized.

The "it takes a village" approach

It's rare if we truly accomplish something all by ourselves. It's important when we've reached a turning point or a point of rediscovery that we share that with those we are closest to. What we often do is fail to tell the most important people in our lives what our goals are and don't find ways to involve them in the process. It's important that they know because as you change they may change or certainly certain aspects of your relationship might change and this needs to be watched for and anticipated.

As you evolve your relationships will evolve.

When you start to change those around you can't help but be changed. The way they interact with you is different and hopefully for the positive. There is a ripple effect and it should be positive if you plan for it to be that way. If you don't plan for it then you will surely run into instances where someone says, "you've changed you're no longer the person that I knew" or something along that line. It will become one of those factors that damage a relationship and it was caused by not communicating.

Another consideration is that people change and evolve at a different pace—things do not move at the same speed for everyone. It's important to share with those closest to you that you want them with you while you go through these changes and afterwards.

People can only do what they know.

You cannot expect people to know what it is that you desire of them if you don't tell them. It's unfair to expect them to read your mind or deal with the changes if you haven't actually communicated to them and worked to make them part of your support and part of the change process itself.

And quite honestly we ourselves sometimes aren't clear in our own understanding of what's going on. We don't always know where we're at emotionally mentally and cognitively. We have to be willing to share that honestly with those we want to maintain a strong relationship with.

Communication with them can be as simple as something like, "I'm not happy. I'm going through something and I really don't know what that is. But I want to change. I want to make things better." Unfortunately most people don't do this consciously or even subconsciously and if we want to maintain strong relationships we have to be willing to communicate openly.

* * *

Sometimes we need something or someone to "open" our eyes and shake us free from our preconceived (or ill-conceived) ideas of what we should do.

There is a story told about three brothers who through the wisdom of their dying father came to understand one of life's truest lessons. I'll share that story (and lesson) with you here:

> There was once a farmer who had a fine olive
> orchard. He was very industrious, and the farm

always prospered under his care. But he knew that his three sons despised the farm work, and were eager to make wealth fast, through adventure.

When the farmer was old, and felt that his time had come to die, he called the three sons to him and said, "My sons, there is a pot of gold hidden in the olive orchard. Dig for it, if you wish it."

The sons tried to get him to tell them in what part of the orchard the gold was hidden; but he would tell them nothing more.

After the farmer was dead, the sons went to work to find the pot of gold; since they did not know where the hiding-place was, they agreed to begin in a line, at one end of the orchard, and to dig until one of them should find the money.

They dug until they had turned up the soil from one end of the orchard to the other, round the tree-roots and between them. But no pot of gold was to be found. It seemed as if someone must have stolen it, or as if the farmer had been wandering in his wits. The three sons were bitterly disappointed to have all their work for nothing.

The next olive season, the olive trees in the orchard bore more fruit than they had ever given before; the fine cultivating they had had from the digging brought so much fruit, and of so fine a quality, that when it was sold it gave the sons a whole pot of gold!

And when they saw how much money had come from the orchard, they suddenly understood what the wise father had meant when he said, "There is gold hidden in the orchard; dig for it."

* * *

Remember life is a journey but a passport isn't a free ride—it's not a free ticket—it's just something that enables you to get to wherever you want to go. You still have to establish the vehicle to get you there.

Chapter 5

Creating A Life Worth Living

"And the day came when the risk to remain tight in a bud was more painful than the risk it took to blossom..."

-Anaïs Nin

It takes commitment and every day counts!

Every day is a stroke of a paint brush that ultimately creates the portrait of our life. It is those who understand this fact and make each day a step forward—a building block—that carries the day's life lesson and supports progress into the next day and on and on. Those who do this become the most effective at mastering the principle of creating a life worth living.

It is not always easy to stop thinking about living long enough to engage in the joy of being alive. There is so much to deal with day in and day out: jobs, careers, relationships, bills to pay and things to do. We can easily be consumed by the routines we establish for our life. Even the pain and hurt of what's wrong or gone wrong becomes a routine. It's the baggage we carry with us and never put down.

We build our sense of joy and a balanced perspective to guide our life based on our ability to take with us the lessons from our yesterdays. And if we keep making our today one full of pain, regrets and recriminations... and the worst thing—inaction or belief we can't change it— then all of our yesterdays will poison the present and future.

Past hurts are vital to making changes in our lives. They should guide you as to what to do... what not to do... what to avoid and what to seek out that you didn't.

You must free yourself from the things that have negative control over you. Your past mistakes, toxic relationships, stereotypes, generational patterns of self-destructive behavior, self-inflicted emotional wounds—these are all demons (small and large) that we create to devil us.

They're the burden we carry that will drag us down or hold us back. And you must let all that old baggage go... put it down, turn squarely to face the truth and acknowledge the past for what it was and is: a lesson to help you build a better future.

Creating commitment in your life requires facing the truth.

Once you face the truth you must live with it while you make the changes necessary to move beyond the past. Commitment leads you to and creates for you a new truth; the truth of the life that you really want and deserve. Living in the truth helps us to appreciate who we are to ourselves and to others around us. Living in the truth we are no longer taken for granted and don't take for granted those around us. Living in the truth acknowledges self-determination, which is one of the main aspects of finding and maintaining commitment. Commitment does not always come easy; neither is keeping it but the struggles make you stronger.

A conversion often comes from that struggle when things line up, when the turning point is encountered and tangible efforts are made. Continuing... to make the commitment takes conviction you are on the right path though that path may be dirty and dusty at first (as unfrequented ones often are). But from dirt and dust God can grow strength and victory.

In the Bible it tells of Paul's turning point and Peter had a turning point, too.

It is not the point of salvation to which I'm speaking but the point to which we say to ourselves, "in spite of what I once was, in spite of what I still need to overcome, in spite of what I am right now... I will live life on purpose."

Saul could have accepted Christ and gone on his way but instead he decided to go through the struggle of proving himself a true follower of Christ.

Peter could have decided to wallow in his many failures as a disciple of Christ but instead he decided to pick himself up from where he was and move on to where he should be. He was committed.

Commitment, simply put, is the will to stand fast or hold in place with unreserved devotion to what you believe is right or good or to do what is necessary to make things right or good in your life, in spite of the circumstances.

We live in a self-serving, throwaway, live-for-the-moment, do-what-feels-good, society. Even in the church those who have professed to know God are committed to their own schemes, goals and desires. But we don't truly benefit until we accept the universality that our spiritual and physical life is connected and each of us individually is also connected as human beings on this Earth. And strong connections help create and sustain commitment.

Joy for the Journey

My grandfather would often say, *"You can tell me where you've been but you can't tell me where you're going!"* And what he said is applicable to many people. The dominant word in any description depicting the spiritual life of a believer in every major world religion is 'journey'. In countless interviews with successful people from all walks of life they mention their life as being a continuum of experience starting when young to present day. The phrase "walks of life" is telling as to how we view a life.

We all have a point we reach from which we must be willing to allow our past to empower our future. This is a simple but timeless truth: when people realize a turning point in their life has come (or is needed), have faith and commit to making the changes needed for a better life... they embark on a journey that will alter them and their life, too. There is an oft repeated quote that, "the journey of a thousand miles begins with the first step."

I'd add to that, "The journey only continues for those who are willing to take the steps, each and every day; one foot in front of the other." That is the essence of commitment and that is what creates the life that you want and we must embrace the journey.

* * *

In 1492 Christopher Columbus set out for the Orient and ended up in the Caribbean. Some believe this started a pattern of behavior, over a span of 500 plus years, which many men still practice today. Some folks simply refuse to stop and ask for directions. Even worse are those who have navigation systems only to question their accuracy. For many people being in a strange place is a challenge and an adventure. Asking for directions spoils the whole fun of the journey. In some cases it may spoil their belief they know where they are going—and have things under control. That last part, that some feel they have things under control so don't need directs, can be a trap that catches us. The fact is that no matter how much you believe you know what you are doing if the results—if you and your life—are not what you want then you are not on the right path. You need to find the right direction to follow.

The Importance of Re-discovery

As we age we often forget the dreams and goals we had as a child, a teen or young adult. As a child we often wish to grow up and be something or like someone that epitomizes a profession that appeals to us. Perhaps it's an astronaut, an actor or athlete that we want to grow up and "do what they do."

Life and circumstances, if we let them, can take those dreams from us or bury them deep... so deep that we forget them or can only painful drag them out their memory for poignant inspection. We turn them over in our mind and nostalgically put them away... no closer to realizing them.

Life does not have to be that way. Your goals and dreams of the past may not be possible or even relevant today. But that doesn't mean you can't set new ones. Ones that are practical and achievable—ones you can start on now—that if you really want them can become a reality. As a grown up this usually means you have to define and prioritize what you need to do for each goal; then work them in order of priority.

What I touch on in this book can be used as a guide to re-discovery. Sorry, there are no short-cuts. But once you realize that it is possible... you will begin. And if what you want to achieve means enough to you... you will hold on to each dream or goal and take the steps. You will do the work to progress towards fulfilling them.

I believe that goals are not some far-off point you are travelling towards you hope one day to reach. They are something you carry with you every day. If they are important to you, you won't put them down or set them aside. Because if you do, the current of life will do one of two things:

1. Wash you away from them, or
2. Wash them away from you.

So you carry them and sometimes they are heavy. But in the carrying you build strength—you build endurance—and that is what gets you to your destination. The point where what you carry no longer weighs anything because it is part of the new you... your new reality.

Here is perhaps some of the wisest advice on doing this:

> "Begin at the beginning and go on
> till you come to the end; then
> stop."

> -Lewis Carroll, Alice in Wonderland

Whether you realize it or not—past-present-future—you are on a journey.

You are reading this book to glean something from it that will help you in some way to take what you have now (life, health or job, etc.) to the next level—making a positive change for you. Or you may be someone who's seeking answers about faith and not yet committed to following a specific religion. Either way, you're on an expedition of discovery. We might work with people who are skeptics or agnostic or atheist or simply not sure what they believe... but they too are on a divine voyage. With the diversity we have in this world the reality is the only common denominator among people is we're all on this trip together trying to figure things out as we go. And along the way the question we each must ask (and answer to ourselves) is: "Am I now where I should be or am I going in the right direction to get there?"

The answer to this question is a primary determinant to putting you on the path to creating the life you want. You must answer it honestly and fully and it's not the type of question that you answer once and are done with it. Life is a series of evaluation and adjustments and creating the life you want requires that you become a watchman.

Chapter 6

Becoming a Watchman (in your own life)

> "Our doubts are traitors, and make us lose the good we oft might win by fearing to attempt."
>
> -William Shakespeare

This circles back to how important it is to find the "honesty" within you. How it is possible to find the person, the soul inside, that represents who you truly are and from that point all the other components of making a positive change in your life reveal to you what you need to do and what road to take.

"I have made you a watchman" Eze. 33:7

A watchman carries a light to shine about and see what surrounds them... what's out there. They are vigilant sentries protecting something of value and watchful for those that might damage or steal it. And the most valuable thing to each of us is what goes on inside our own head—what's the nature and tone of our inner dialogue.

Controlling your mental diet

It's human to be influenced by those around you. The problem develops when that impact is out of balance and affects you negatively to a larger or lesser degree. Friends family or coworkers that are negative, are eternally pessimistic or sad and always unhappy can and will drag you down. It's important to know when to separate yourself from people like that.

They can remain friends or family and you can coexist with them as a coworker but you must control how much their pessimism or their personalities affect you. You have to watch closely the conversations you have with them because what happens (the damage to you) is very subtle. It's nothing that happens overnight or a drastic change. Slowly, inexorably, you find yourself drawn into their negativity and it can become a downward spiral.

Humans change incrementally and just as you can improve your life bit-by-bit, without a doubt there are things and people that become like the death of a thousand cuts. Each slice cuts away part of your spirit and makes your life much less than it could or should be.

It's important to constantly monitor what and who you're listening to day in and day out. If it's a constant litany of ranting or of sadness, of desperation and negativity how in the world can that positively help you? What good does that serve?

If you have people around you that fall into that category you need to distance yourself from them. It's not a matter of feeling superior or acting as if you are better than them. You have to make a choice the same way you decide what your body feeds on. What your mind feeds on is very important and something that a lot of people don't understand and don't realize.

Choose a healthy mental diet.

* * *

It's been said the definition of insanity is, "to do the same things in the same way and to expect a different outcome."

Humans are creatures of habit. We are most comfortable with those things that we are most familiar. That is the path of least resistance and something you must overcome if you do want to bring about a change in your life.

One of the things most constant in life is change. But it's up to the individual to mold and shape the outcome of the change that occurs. If we don't exert some measure of control then what happens is a life full of inadvertent events. And just like plants can grow wild, teeth grow crooked and hair become unruly without trimming or barbering... so can a life.

Outcomes

The outcome of a decision or indecision is always something that should be a planning consideration.

Many people get a job and never think about what happens if they lose that job or what happens if they don't like the job. How do you get out of it or how do you recover from it with the least amount of damage so that you're in good position to move forward with another opportunity. CEOs of large companies are very smart and they do this all the time. The most intelligent people have this conversation first with themselves and then with their employer very early on. They negotiate or prepare themselves so that if the outcome is not what they expect they land on their feet often with a very good severance package or certainly in a position or with an opening or opportunity to get a comparable or perhaps even better position with another company. People that don't think about these things often find themselves at a disadvantage and if such an event occurs at an inopportune time it can have devastating effect on someone's life.

Managing the change, controlling and guiding it, to your advantage can be uncomfortable. It can be a challenge but if you want to have control of your life you must do these things. And one thing that you must understand even if you embrace change and set goals and in the things designed to improve your life; life requires maintenance.

You can't make it a simple or single decision and not have to make a course correction or adjustments along the way. The analogy of the purpose of braces on your teeth is appropriate. When you're fitted with braces its uncomfortable and often painful. Over time those braces have to be adjusted so that the goal is met. The end result is an improved set of teeth. It's like that, in life, too. We have to make adjustments. We have to gage how we're doing and if something seems off course or out of alignment we make corrections as we go.

Now, here's the challenge you need to strive to meet and accept. You can bear the pain. You can bear the discomfort. But only if you know the result is worthwhile. It has to be crystal clear in your mind that the result is in fact worthwhile. The good thing is for those who meet and accept that challenge they inevitably say that the pain and the work was well worth it. It's a long-term perspective.

Becoming a watchman means not just outward awareness but also looking deep inside you to determine:

- who you are,
- what you are seeking,

- is what you seek what you need;
- that you are not alone, and
- how to discover your turning point;
- a better world for yourself and others
- and building a life that you want to live.

And so you must shine a light on your life and what it consists of.

Your life is yours to be accountable for and responsible to and you must watch as it unfolds and make adjustments as needed.

REMEMBER WE ARE OUR BROTHERS KEEPER BUT WE ARE ALSO RESPONSIBLE FOR OURSELVES.

Just as a ship from the time it leaves port must adjust its course, because of the forces of wind and sea, in order to reach its destination; life is series of adjustments and refinement—sometimes of purpose and sometimes of method—for it to be what we want it to be.

* * *

A Point of Light in Every Soul

by Dennis Lowery

There's a point of light in every soul
that can reveal a path to follow.
It may be a trail that twists and turns.

And at times can feel like you've lost the way.
But the light reveals more as you go.
And you will see more of yourself with every step.
To see sights and scenes you would never witness.
If you had not pushed beyond the dark.
Beyond the bend in the trail.

Man is more than mind and body. We are also spirit. That part of you that pushes you on when the mind shuts down and the body wants to give up. It can't be touched with human hands but we all know that it's there. God did not give us a spirit of fear... he gave us one of love and power to control our own destiny.

When we discover this for our own life and have "walked the walk" of improving our self then often comes a desire (and perhaps a responsibility) to help others do the same.

Overseeing, leading guiding others effectively requires a level of self-worth, and love that appreciates the divine in you and in others.

But you can't be respected as a person worth listening to if you have done little to help yourself and you cannot change others just by wishing them to do so. They, too, have to realize if for themselves. But you can give them your own example... show them your own experience.

The one thing I am certain about is that good begets good and wisdom begets wisdom. The truly good people are the lights of the world. They are watchman not only for themselves but through their enlightenment also work to light the path for others. Within such enlightenment is the seed of wisdom. There are three determining facts that let you know if you are truly on the path of wisdom (and all necessary to become a watchman in your life):

First you need to know that the journey of life is one of FAITH.

The Bible says of the saints, "We walk by faith and not by sight." This is true of the wise because what you see may not always be what it looks like! The question was asked

"Where is He who has been born King of the Jews? For we have seen His star in the East." Not everyone was able first of all to recognize His star. Next, the wise were walking in faithful anticipation of what was about to occur when they saw Him. Lastly, they didn't walk towards Him to simply get something from Him... but to get what they had to Him.

What would prompt someone to leave the comfort of their homes to go on a dangerous journey? Somebody said, "Romance." Well maybe for a short while. Somebody said, "Wealth." Well, money can buy you a lot but there are still some things money just can't buy.

But faith? Yes! Faith can prompt you and more importantly can sustain you on any journey.

"Where is He who has been born the King of the Jews?" What a probing question; there is no doubt in their language that He had been born. The question is "Where is He?" They had seen the star—the evidence was real—now where is He? They had faith that He was alive; that He existed. Now all they needed to do was to find Him. Their purpose was established—find Him. And so they were willing to risk everything. They were willing to leave the safety of their homes and risk a perilous journey to seek a King.

This was all about Faith! Can you imagine their neighbor's reaction? "Are you going on a journey?" "Yes." "Where are you going?" "We don't know for sure." "How far is it?"

"Well we don't know that either." How long are you going to be gone?" Well were not quite sure on that either." "Boy for wise men you sure don't much do you?"

And so it may be for many of us who have gone on our own journeys—without answering every question—compelled to go by a power and sense of purpose.

The world will always attempt to stop the progress of the faithful. They said similar things to Abraham when he left his home for the Promised Land. They must have said the same things to Noah who was building an ark even though it had never rained in the history of the earth up till that point. They must have said the same kind of things to Peter, Andrew, John and James when they left their fishing nets to become fishers of men, "What are you crazy? Are you insane? Are you out of your minds?" But they were not crazy—not insane—not out of their minds—they were men of faith.

Transformational journeys always involve FAITH.

People of faith have been willing to respond to the challenges of the unknown over and over again down through history.

William Cary was a shoemaker when one day he heard of the millions of people in India who had not heard the Good News of Jesus Christ. He believed the great commission to "Go into all the world and preach the gospel." He believed that that verse was speaking directly to him. So he volunteered to go to India but was told "Young man, sit down. When God wants to convert the heathen, He will do it without your help." Cary went anyway—supporting himself. For seven years he worked without seeing a single convert—but by the end of his life he saw hundreds of churches and thousands of converts. Today he is known as the "Father of Modern Missions." He was a man of faith.

Second, a wise person's journey is one of COMMITMENT.

When the wise men went on their journey it was for the purpose of worship. They were committed to following the Star in the East and the belief that it signified the birth of the King of the Jews... the Son of God. And so they brought with them gifts of gold, frankincense and myrrh. These gifts have a lot of symbolism associated with them. Gold represents wealth. It is a gift fit for a king (Jesus was the King of Kings). Frankincense is the sap of a tree that was dried and hardened and used as incense to worship God. Thus we see a gift for his deity. (Jesus was the Son of God). Myrrh is a fragrant perfume that was used to anoint the dead—to embalm and preserve them. (Jesus was The Sacrificial Lamb). But there is more to worship then gold, frankincense, or myrrh isn't there? And you can never reach any destination without commitment to get there.

There is always a requirement of time and effort, a sacrifice you make for COMMITMENT.

Was there a price to be paid for the wise men's worship? You bet. They had given themselves to a journey. Travel in those days was not very comfortable—in fact it could be downright dangerous. The wise men had sacrificed their own comfort to find the king and worship Him. Listen to what David said about sacrifice:

"I will not offer to the Lord my God burnt offerings that cost [me] nothing." 2 Samuel 24:24 (HCSB).

To be truly committed to making a change in your life requires sacrifice. Nothing comes easy and certainly the value of becoming the person you wish to be, to having the life that you want, is going to require more from you than just wishes and dreams.

The third point I want to make this is your life's journey is one of CHANGE.

"Then, being divinely warned in a dream that they (the three wise men) should not return to Herod, they departed for their own country another way."

The desire for change begins the stirrings... the ripples that can have far reaching effect and we may never be the "same". We may never return to our "life" the same way that we got to where we are.

I used the word "transformational" above as it relates to the journey you undertake when your faith is driving you to a destination. But I have to confess something here. I believe that sometimes change is not necessarily making yourself "different" as much as it is figuring out who you truly are and then re-shaping the world around you.

I believe that being honest, especially with one's self, is the foundation of a free and unencumbered soul. Every human being is a work in progress... and it is incremental. Minute by minute, hour by hour, day by day... and so it goes on. Make time count, be honest and become who you really are... who you want to be: as a person, as a parent, as a citizen of the world.

I believe the essence of each person resides in their soul... what type of person they are... what kind of experiences they've had... how they treat people... how people treat them... do they give love... and are they loved. And many other things, the bits and pieces that make us who we are.

None of us is a perfect soul. There is good and bad in all of us, each with their own unique balance of the two. We've all done stupid things in our lives and possibly will do more as life continues to unfold. But there are also brilliant moments... bright shining accomplishments, moments and times of grace and beauty, that strike us deeply at our core. To strive for the good, for the grace, for the beauty that can be had in life... to deal with and persevere through the bad, through the awkward, through the ugly moments and events—these are all part of the human existence. How we act and how we respond to these experiences shapes our soul. And the shaping of our soul is the true duty of a watchman.

BREATHE DEEP

by Dennis Lowery

We breathe shallow
When we should breathe deep
We fall
When we should stand
Our dreams lay fallow
But they are ours to keep
The call
Is heard
The time is at hand
Rise
And breathe deep

To the End

Perhaps we should refer to a classic line from Paul McCartney and make a slight change from, *'And in the end, the love you get is equal to the love you give'*... to this:

"And in the end, the life you get is equal to the life you make."

There are two important final points to make:

1. We all have an expiration date. No one knows how long they have on this Earth. What we do with the time we do have is what matters.
2. There is a difference between existing and living.

These two points are affected by the three things that make up a human being:

1. **Mind**
2. **Body**
3. **Spirit**

At different points in our life we look at those three components through distinctly different lenses. As we all know, a lens is used to help us see something more distinctly. It can bring what is far away closer to our view. It can make very tiny things larger and easier to see. It can take what is fuzzy or unclear and focus to bring it sharply into our view.

Lenses, in the purest sense, provide clarity.

Physically we know that as we age our eyesight dims. It's usually not quite as good as it was when we were young(er). But spiritually, as we age, our 'sight' and understanding should be much more powerful and better able to see things clearly that reflect on and affect our soul.

Here is something that might put this in better context:

A woman was caught committing adultery and the punishment was stoning. As the crowd gathered with stones in their hands, Jesus realized that the situation may have been intended as a test for him. As they approached, some in the crowd asked him, as the Rabbi, as the teacher, what should be done to her? He had been preaching love and forgiveness and they wanted to know what should be done to this person who had transgressed—this person who had broken one of their social laws.

Jesus didn't immediately answer them though they continued to press the question. As the crowd got louder and more demanding Jesus stooped and wrote something in the sand—we don't know what but perhaps it was just a means to clarify his thoughts for a moment. The crowd seemed to sense that perhaps he could not or would not answer them and got even louder—more aggressive. As they crowded closer, Jesus stood and said "let him among you without sin cast the first stone." And this stopped them in their tracks as each, in their own way, considered and gave thought to that statement.

What some people overlook in this text or passage is what surely happened next. Some in the crowd dropped their stones and stepped away from the others and what's important to note is that it was the older people in the crowd that dropped their stones first. They had lived longer and were guilty of questionable actions themselves. They had more at stake.

The interpretation of this, I believe, is that they freed themselves by dropping their stones. They learned something important about themselves.

Often when we're hurt... when we're angry... we lash out. We reach for a stone to cast... something to throw even if the thing that we want to throw it at is ourselves.

There is a bit of a paradox we face.

When judging others. The younger we are the more likely we are to be extremely harsh in our judgment—idealistic and even intolerant. The older we are the more balanced should be our perspective. We've lived longer. Seen and done more. We know more of life's (and peoples) imperfections, inadequacies and the often irrational nature of events.

When judging our self. The younger we are the more likely we are to be easier on ourselves. Some young people think, "It's not a big deal" and don't understand the consequences of their actions (or inaction). The older we are the harsher we are (and should be). We do know the lessons of cause and effect. We do know there is a price paid later in life for the decisions made (not made) today.

So if you, the reader, are a young person—take to heart the message that it's very important to be self-aware of what happens as a result of the decisions you make or don't make in life. If you are an older person—take to heart that you probably know and can do better... so just do it.

And that is largely the goal of this book: to help the reader find clarity in life in order to put things in proper perspective and to make things better. Success and happiness in life requires the following "must haves" to progress towards reaching them:

- Clarity of what you want
- Clarity of relevance
- Clarity of purpose
- Clarity of steps to take

Much of success in life and all its facets (job, profession and personal) are determined by how well you do your front end work. By front-end I mean how well you prepare, how well you do in evaluating, assessing and understanding your current situation, where you want to go or what you want to accomplish and the steps to get there. That takes thought and frankly some people don't want to take the time to do that and that's why they end up with less than acceptable results.

What I've touched on in this book is not a magic formula that will solve everyone's problems and improve everyone's life. Like anything knowledge is good, education is important but it is action that dictates the result.

It's important to understand that many of the things we discussed and touched on need to be molded and shaped to conform to the context of your life. Not everyone is the same, we are each unique and so must be the circumstances that we find ourselves facing.

There are some common themes and issues that we as humans must address but each solution and approach can be somewhat different. When it comes to the human condition and its complexity there is not a cookie-cutter solution that applies to all of us. It's up to each of us to look at the tools and the knowledge that is available and adapt for our own use so that we generate the best possible result for ourselves.

Use this book to generate thought applicable in the context of your situation and who you are and to develop a strategy that works for you. This is something that is relevant for you today and it will be relevant for you tomorrow and five or ten years from now.

There is one thing that is certain. As we age and gain experience our perspectives change and sometimes our needs change with our increased abilities and experience level. That's why it's important to instill a constant state of self-awareness. Awareness of where you are, who you are what you want to do and what you want to be at that point in time so that you can adjust your course as you go.

The process never ends and you have to be ever vigilant and ever certain that your life rest's in your hands—others may be of help but creating the life you want is your responsibility. And in keeping with that thought here is something that has inspired people for over one hundred years. It's an excerpt from the speech "*Citizenship In A Republic*" given by Theodore Roosevelt, 26th President of the United States of America, at the Sorbonne, in Paris, France on 23 April, 1910.

"It is not the critic who counts; not the man who points out how the strong man stumbles, or where the doer of deeds could have done them better. The credit belongs to the man who is actually in the arena, whose face is marred by dust and sweat and blood; who strives valiantly; who errs, who comes short again and again, because there is no effort without error and shortcoming; but who does actually strive to do the deeds; who knows great enthusiasms, the great devotions; who spends himself in a worthy cause; who at the best knows in the end the triumph of high achievement, and who at the worst, if he fails, at least fails while daring greatly, so that his place shall never be with those cold and timid souls who neither know victory nor defeat."

The credit belongs to you for living life and not letting it live you. The honor goes to those who strive; who work and labor to build something better in their lives for themselves and those around them.

Ultimately life is truly about the choices you make.

To a large extent these choices are formed by what you believe and that is based on what you feed your mind on a daily basis.

Below are a few time tested thoughts, to encourage your life path, that have been empowering for many others on their journey of self-enlightenment and truth:

2 Timothy 4:7-8

New International Version (NIV)

⁷ I have fought the good fight, I have finished the race, I have kept the faith. ⁸ Now there is in store for me the crown of righteousness, which the Lord, the righteous Judge, will award to me on that day—and not only to me, but also to all who have longed for his appearing.

Philippians 3:12-13

New International Version (NIV)

¹² Not that I have already obtained all this, or have already arrived at my goal, but I press on to take hold of that for which Christ Jesus took hold of me. ¹³ Brothers and sisters, I do not consider myself yet to have taken hold of it. But one thing I do: Forgetting what is behind and straining toward what is ahead,

Hebrews 12:1-3

New King James Version (NKJV)

The Race of Faith
¹² Therefore we also, since we are surrounded by so great a cloud of witnesses, let us lay aside every weight, and the sin which so easily ensnares *us,* and let us run with endurance the race that is set before us, ² looking unto Jesus, the author and finisher of *our* faith, who for the joy that was set before Him endured the cross, despising the

shame, and has sat down at the right hand of the throne of God.

CPSIA information can be obtained at www.ICGtesting.com
Printed in the USA
LVOW121206170313

324627LV00007B/634/P